SO YOU REALLY WANT TO SUE YOUR DOCTOR! HERE'S WHEN AND HOW YOU MAY DO IT.
Medical Malpractice 101.

By Roy T. Rapp, M.D.

Library of Congress Cataloging-in-Publication Data

Rapp, Roy T.
    So you really want to sue your doctor: here's when and how you may do it:: medical
malpractice 101 / by Roy T. Rapp.
        p.   cm.
    Includes bibliographical references and index.
     ISBN 0-932704-72-7
    1.   Physicians--Malpractice--United States--Popular works. I. Title.
    KF2905. 3 . Z9R37 2005
    344 . 7304 ' 121– dc22

                                        2005044860

Printed in the United States of America
ISBN: 0-932704-72-7
Library of Congress Catalog Number:

Published by:
Do-It-Yourself Legal Publishers

27 Edgerton Terrace
East Orange, NJ 07017

DEDICATION

I dedicate this book to *Cornelius Henninger*, O.F.M, who was my science teacher in high school, then college professor, my role model, and just a good person, who always did the right thing and was available to counsel and help those in need.

Father Cornelius was responsible for imprinting in me the label of a vocation, rather than a profession, for what a physician does.

On one occasion, the President of St. Louis University visited our college. Fr. Cornelius, apparently impressed with my character and academic achievements, arranged it, making it turn out that I was the only student invited to the luncheon for the guest. I was introduced as a worthy possible recipient of a scholarship to St. Louis University School of Medicine. This did not happen, but not because Fr. Cornelius did not try.

God loved him, and so did I. I hope I did not disappoint him.

Father Cornelius

ACKNOWLEDGMENT

My son, James A. Rapp, J.D., a practicing Illinois attorney and author, is the writer I strive to imitate. He is the successful author of a well-regarded legal series titled, *Education Law,* published by the major national law text publisher, Matthew Bender. He is also the principal author of the series, *Medical Malpractice in Illinois, Medical Malpractice in Pennsylvania, and Medical Malpractice in Texas, all* published by the Mosby Company, and numerous other publications.

For this book, with his permission, I have drawn liberally from these and his other publications, as well as from liberal consultations with him. And for all these, I remain deeply grateful and indebted to him.

I am not an attorney. I have diligently endeavored to be factual and technically accurate in the information presented in the book. Nevertheless, there may, quite possibly, be some errors or inaccuracies in the book, in regard particularly to the technical aspects of the law and the practice of medical malpractice lawsuit procedures. Hopefully, they will not be too many, or of much seriousness. Nevertheless, where such errors occur, again I alone am completely responsible for them.

I must also express my sincere gratitude and thankfulness to **Judy M. Hackworth**, my able Writing Assistant and aide, who worked tirelessly with me in the assembling of the facts and research information necessary in the writing of this book, and in aspects of its writing and editing, and in working with the publisher.

However, whatever errors the book contains, they are attributable solely to me.

I welcome corrections or observations and comments.

My sincere gratitude and appreciation go, as well, to the Publisher and its staff, particularly Dr. Benjamin Anosike, Ph.D., the Editor on the book, for the great job of editing and refinement done on the book which have contributed appreciably in making the book yet a better work for the readers.

--Roy T. Rapp, M.D.

WRITING, DESIGN, AND GRAPHICS CREDITS

Editor and formatting designer of the book, Benjamin O. Anosike, Ph.D.

Researcher, Writing Assistant to author, Judy M. Hackworth

Illustrator, graphics work, J. B. Elmore

Illustrator J.B. Elmore with a portrait that he did of our clinic manager, Margie Thompson.

The Publisher's Disclaimer

It remains for us, the Publishers, to assure our readers that we have diligently researched, checked and counterchecked every bit of the information contained in this book to ensure its accuracy and up-to-dateness. Nevertheless, we humans have never been noted for our infallibility, no matter how hard the effort! Furthermore, details of laws, rules, or procedures dealing with virtually any subject matter or topic, do change from time to time, and, oftentimes, even the laws themselves do differ in particular specifics and details, from state to state. That reality is not different for medical malpractice issues and the delivery of health care services addressed by this book. Indeed, if anything, the issue of constant, even rapid changes, are particularly true and applicable with respect to the field of medicine. Nor is this relatively short manual conceivable intended to be an encyclopedia on the subject containing the answer or solution to every issue on the subject

THE READER IS THEREFORE FOREWARNED THAT THIS MANUAL IS SOLD AND DISTRIBUTED WITH THIS DISCLAIMER: The publisher (and/or the author) does not make any promises or guarantees of any kind whatsoever, or purport to engage in rendering professional or legal service, or to substitute for a lawyer, an accountant, financial or social advisor, or the like. Where such professional help is legitimately called for in your own specific or other cases, it should be sought accordingly.

~Do-It-Yourself Legal Publishers

TABLE OF CONTENTS

CHAPTER I

A FEW 'HORROR'STORIES

CHAPTER II

WHAT CONSTITUTES TRUE MEDICAL MALPRACTICE UNDER LAW?

CHAPTER III

THE MAIN REASONS FOR WHICH PHYSICIANS GET SUED?

CHAPTER IV

THE PRELIMINARY INVOLVEMENT OF AN ATTORNEY IN A MEDICAL MALPRACTICE CASE

CHAPTER V

CERTAIN PRELIMINARY PROCEDURES THAT MAY TAKE PLACE BEFORE A LAWSUIT IS ACTUALY INSTITUTED

CHAPTER VI

THE LAWSUIT IS FILED: THE BATTLE BEGINS

CHAPTER VII

PRE-TRIAL SKIRMISHES

CHAPTER VIII

THE TRIAL

CHAPTER IX

ARE THERE LEGITIMATE SITUATIONS & INSTANCES
WHEN ONE'S DOCTOR OUGHT TO BE SUED? SURE!

APPENDICES

FOREWORD to the book

By Benjamin O. Anosike, Ph.D.

Book is Balanced: Neither For/Against The Doctor, Or The Patient or His Lawyer

What is a venerable, professionally well-fulfilled, eminent American family physician and abdominal surgeon doing writing a how-it-is-done manual on medical malpractice lawsuit making in America? This is probably the first thought, if wonderment, that will grip the average reader who glances at this title, *SO YOU REALLY WANT TO SUE YOUR DOCTOR!* Admittedly an intriguing thought, alright, since medical malpractice and malpractice trial attorneys have arguably become the 'Great Satan' that have harassed and even terrorized the doctors engaged in the great American health care delivery system in recent times! And, surely, at first glance, the book sounds like it is an encouragement, even an invitation, for patients to sue their doctors, and a do-it-yourself manual on how to do it.

You might, even if for a brief fleeting moment, be tempted to think so. However, what you'll find is this. That, as you begin to go through the actual contents of the book, you'll quickly come to another mystifying realization: although it bemoans the state of the American medical malpractice litigation war today, and invites both the embittered, sore doctor, as well as the litigious medical patient and his rapacious, greedy plaintiffs' lawyer, to 'knock it off,' there is an underlying subliminal message that rings loudly through the book, saying to the patient, "proceed with extreme care and caution on this; what is actually involved in this whole malpractice lawsuit business may be a lot more intricate than you've probably been led to believe; there is a lot more to it than simply running to a lawyer and a courthouse and yelling 'malpractice' 'malpractice,' and expecting automatically to leave with a ton of quick, easy money from your doctor."

Though the book's author is a career physician, it is a physician of a unique and special kind that's involved in this case: a physician and surgeon of the finest quality who clearly has a real, genuine, and unselfish interest in what is best, not simply for himself or his fellow doctors, but equally for his thousands of medical patients of over 50 years, as well as even for the people, the lawyers, themselves, who practice malpractice law against his fellow physicians, all the same. *Consequently, what we have in this book by Dr. Roy T. Rapp, is a unique and balanced book which successfully bridges the disturbingly growing and inhospitable gap between the physician, the patient, and the trial lawyers involved in America's contemporary medical malpractice tug-of-war.*

Americans Are In Common Agreement That the Health Care Delivery System Is Broken

Americans are customarily of divided, or, at least, different opinions as to the actual nature or causes for the current state of gridlock in the nation's health care system. Is it because of its cost, and the fact that it could often be high or unaffordable? Is it because of the ugly handiwork of those doctors within the profession, who are truly incompetent, though tiny in number, and the highly sensationalized 'horror' stories that are often portrayed in the media about outrageous instances of doctoring by such doctors? Is it because of the unrealistic or perfectionist expectations of American patients which often have them demanding or expecting a 'perfect' cure or outcome in the treatment of their medical conditions? Is it because of the greed of the legal industry and the rapacious malpractice attorneys who build lucrative legal careers on the backs of the medical misfortunes of doctors and patients alike? Is it because of the proliferation of bogus malpractice cases by unconscionable plaintiffs' attorneys who file junk, frivolous lawsuits for the sake of reaping a bonanza? Is it because of the over-sophistication of the medical system, and the overspecialization and consequent segmentation of medical practice by unnecessary specialization among American doctors and other health care providers, which, according to Dr. Rapp and others, now has the doctors "knowing more and more about less and less," and have them treating the patients as 'parts,' and not as an integrated 'whole,' to further contribute to the escalation in the cost of medical and surgical care? And so on and on?

Opinions about what is believed to be the true causes or reasons for the mess in today's American health care system, or even about who are to be blamed for it, can stretch on and on in variation, almost as varied in number as the views on how to fix the problem. However, that's just about the only area about which there is a variation in views. For, on the other hand, *on one thing virtually all sides in the debate are completely agreed upon, and that is that the system, the American health care delivery system, is in a genuine, serious crisis and urgent need for reformation!*

Damage Of the Present Malpractice System To Health Care, Patients & Doctors
Evidence, for example, of massive systemic malfunction in medical malpractice is starting to accumulate. For starters, according to studies reported only recently in the *Business Week* of March 2005, only 2% of the people who are genuinely injured in a medical treatment or procedure, even bother to file lawsuits, believing that the system is just too bloated. For those people who brave going to court, only 40% of every dollar spent on litigation goes to the victims. Then, there's the spreading damage to the doctors that's now beginning to be widely recognized and acknowledged as real. For example, for some specialists, such as those practicing in the so-called 'high-risk' specialties, such as obstetrics and some surgical areas, doctors' premiums for medical malpractice insurance costs doctors anywhere from 20% to 50% of their annual income, according to reliable estimates. That's why these days' specialists like obstetricians, neurosurgeons, and orthopedic surgeons, are avoiding trauma cases, and/or eliminating emergency calls. Indeed, many medical practitioners involved in such high risk specialties, often owing primarily because they can't afford the high cost of malpractice insurance associated with their practice, have quit their profession altogether.

As one major byproduct, such drumbeat of problems has driven an unfortunate wedge of suspicion and acrimony between the doctors and the health care providers, on the one hand, and the patients and their plaintiffs' attorneys, on the other hand, often leading the doctors today, most unfortunately, "to regard every patient [with suspicion] as a potential litigant, and [to] try to shield themselves by practicing 'defensive medicine,' thus further exacerbating the problem even more for the average patient in terms of escalating the cost of health care." Author Roy T. Rapp emphasizes, again and again, that *ultimately, in all of this, it is the American patients, themselves, who wind up in the end paying for these problems in terms of the higher and higher costs and inconveniences of medical care they'd have to incur as the average patient!*

Book Skillfully Integrates Both the Legal and Medical Aspects of the Problem
But what, then, is the real solution to this nagging problem, what is to be done? The differential, if unique contribution of Dr. Rapp's *SO YOU REALLY WANT TO SUE YOUR DOCTOR!* is that it attempts to get at the problem, and its root causes and possible solution, via a different, rather unorthodox, way,

namely, by way of providing a rare, even unprecedented insider's 'window' into the problem – i.e., from the perspective both of the medical practitioner in the field, and of the patient, and the legal practitioners, themselves, and how, in practical terms, these major players in the issue actually operate and interact in the medical malpractice litigation tug-of-war.

Dr. Rapp's book, quite clearly displays the hallmark of one competent professional (a medical doctor) who could readily borrow quite proficiently from another group of professionals (the lawyers), albeit the ones who are homegrown "from the family," namely, his five lawyer-sons. Quite strikingly, the book reads like a competent Law 101 primer in the art of medical malpractice lawsuit-making and the practical mechanics and step-by-step dynamics of the doctor-patient courtroom trials and procedures. *It does such a great job of it, outlining the practical ins and outs of medical malpractice lawsuits and how it all works, both from the doctor's as well as the patient's sides, that any party whosoever who has a primary interest in the subject – physicians, nurses and other medical care providers, hospitals, patients or their relations, malpractice attorneys, etc – will find this book to be such a great instructional and information goldmine on the how-tos of filing and processing a medical malpractice lawsuit, or defending against it.*

Yet, the book is not so much a legal primer in the 'how-it-is-or-should-be-done' of medical malpractice lawsuits, as it is a primer in how and when NOT to do it, or, even more relevantly, how and when to do it the RIGHT and the PROPER WAY – when it is legitimate and where it is legitimate to do it. Put another way, this book is more than just a how-to manual on how the medical malpractice lawsuit is done, or even how it should be done, or more properly done. *Rather, it is a medical-legal-sociological text on how, effectively, to reform the present gridlocked American medical malpractice system, which is largely fueled by patients who, generally by reason of their inducement by their malpractice attorneys, often think that the only real recourse that a patient has for redressing a medical wrong or injury, is a malpractice lawsuit against the doctor or hospital.*

Argues For A Different Remedy That Gets Rid of the Bad Doctors

The author argues, quite persuasively and cogently, that while it is fully understandable that some disaffected patients, angered and frustrated by the professional excesses or outright failures or incompetence of their doctors or hospitals, may naturally want to seek remedy by resorting to the courts, the present system of purported remedy by suing the doctors for money, still winds up in the end providing the aggrieved patient, even if with a legitimate cause, no real "remedy," in that such present courtroom, money-based "remedy," still leaves unresolved what is really the primary interest and desire of the American patients (though, obviously, not necessarily of his or her malpractice trial attorney!), which is a substantial improvement of the quality of health care for him or her. And what is more ominous, the author adds, such existing courtroom-oriented patient "remedy" might wind up even wrecking the whole American health care delivery industry altogether for EVERY patient, and to the detriment of every patient, if allowed to continue and not urgently reformed and corrected.

Quite interestingly, *SO YOU REALLY WANT TO SUE YOUR DOCTOR!* does not contend that there are no situations or instances when it is legitimate or warranted that the doctor should be sued. Not at all! Quite to the contrary, the author stresses that the right of the patient, when genuinely injured, to sue his/her doctor, should be preserved, emphasizing that there are "good, bad and careless physicians." The author is quick to admit that "a few (incompetent physicians) who are below average have squeezed into the profession," but emphasizes that such physicians "that fail the Oath of Hippocrates, should be dispatched with aplomb" from the practice of medicine or the treating of patients.

Dr. Rapp, the respected-family-doctor-turned-author, is perhaps at one of his most persuasive positions when he sums up the book's central point of view in the following language: "there are occasions and circumstances when a patient should sue his/her doctor for malpractice. Absolutely! However, ...it is imperative that patients be absolutely certain that they have precisely that kind of a situation before they rush to court for such legal 'remedy.' Or, perhaps more accurately, before they allow themselves to be stampeded into running to the courts by rapacious trial lawyers who dominate the increasingly lucrative American medical malpractice industry! In the final analysis, the critical point for the patient, for America today, is this: is this current courtroom 'remedy' really the permanent, sustainable, workable solution to the American health care crisis? Has it brought the patient any closer to relief for their primary need and interest in health care – improvement in the quality of health care for them? That is, could we be throwing out the baby (the entire health care system, which we all profess to desire), with the bath water (a few dollars for a handful of patients, and lots of it for the greedy lawyers)?"

Some Specific Reform Proposals For The Medical Malpractice Problem
The specific reforms or remedies for licking the problem? Dr. Rapp offers quite a few intriguing ones. He proposes that America should begin to think seriously about the rationing of medical services. He further proposes replacing the present medical malpractice system with a new system that places a cap on the court awards that could be granted for malpractice claims, and a new system that will screen out and shut down or rid the incompetent doctors, by suspension and revocation of their license to practice medicine, arguing that it sounds to reason that "if you consider the person (your doctor), who you say has done all these awful things to you and your life, to be really as bad and terrible as your lawyer's complaint says he is, then you should want to put that 'terrible' person out of business! Instead of demanding tons of money award as your 'remedy,' why not seek to petition the State officials to take away that doctor's license to practice so that he cannot injure you or anyone else ever?"

This is, quite probably, a good omen, possibly presaging the actual commencement of progress on this vital issue. The Rapp proposals for medical malpractice reform are closely in keeping with a rising outcry in recent times in the nation for a complete overhaul of the ignominious "tort" system, of which the medical malpractice is just a part. Indeed, in recent times many physicians, lawyers, and politicians, have called for the creation of the European-type idea of special 'Health Courts.' Once thought of as 'too radical' for America, such courts, as in many Western-European countries, would be manned by dedicated, administrative judges with special orientations, a panel of neutral experts, and medically trained staff. Pretrial court "discovery" procedures would be limited, and the cases will be tried, not by a jury, but by the special judges, thereby the cost of filing malpractice cases would be considerably less. By this system, it is expected, more injured people would be induced to make claims, and more importantly, they would get their award money faster, and a greater share of it will go into their own pockets, rather than their lawyers'. But here is the trade-off: there will be no 'emotional' or 'punitive' damages awards. To ensure awards consistency, the Health Court awards would be based simply on a European-style damages schedule. Thus, in Britain, for example, damages award paid for quadriplegia (a matter which will be a sure banker for tens of millions of dollars in an American malpractice case), will range from $311,000 to $387,000, depending on a patient's residual movement, depression, pain and age.

Indeed, already, segments of America, from doctors' groups and plaintiffs' trial attorneys, to business, labor, the Congress and President Bush, seem to be heeding the serious call of *SO YOU REALLY WANT TO SUE YOUR DOCTOR!* For example, tort reform is high on America's political agenda this year for the first time in years. In this 2005 year alone, a proposal, called *Lawsuit Abuse Reduction Act*, is in the works, which would fine lawyers who file frivolous lawsuits and require judges to refer repeat violators for disciplinary action. There is a legislative bill proposal now in Congress which would limit pain-and-suffering payout at $250,000, cap attorneys' fees, and require the courts to reduce the compensation awards for expenses already covered by health insurance, and the like. And many more others.

Why the Author and His Remedies Are Uniquely & Immediately Credible

In the final analysis, when it's all said and done, there is, ultimately, probably no "perfect" solution for the medical malpractice problem for everyone, as there is no perfect way to balance the disparate interests of everybody who has a stake in the ongoing medical malpractice (and tort reform) debate. But Dr. Rapp's SO YOU REALLY WANT TO SUE YOUR DOCTOR!, is a major contribution of a unique kind to this important national debate. Its major asset lies in its distinctive *credibility*, a credibility that is, in turn, borne out of its author's *credibility*.

Roy T. Rapp is a somewhat rare, if unique, member of the medical profession of note. He is not one who might have been embittered or aggrieved by some previous malpractice lawsuits or accusations against him at the hands of his patients, being that he has never had even one patient lawsuit in his over 50 years of service to his patients, but has been, rather, a doctor widely beloved by the patients he has so well served, and vice versa. On top of that, he has been, by extension and family affiliation, a 'member' of the legal profession, as well – five out of his six children in his beloved, closely knit family, are attorneys, some of whom have been involved in medical malpractice law practice. (One of those five, is both a physician and an attorney, but mainly practices medicine). Thus, as a writer of SO *YOU REALLY WANT TO SUE YOUR DOCTOR!,* author Roy T. Rapp is without peer as one with no particular bias or axe to grind on the subject matter, he is with no particular chip on his shoulders, or any particular political or professional agenda or self-interest to push, but comes across as one, as a writer, who has come to the subject matter out of a genuine altruistic desire to tell the story, and to give the facts of the matter, exactly 'like it is' – without fear or favor, without partisanship, selfishness or bitterness.

Why This Book Comes Highly Recommended

This is why, when author Rapp recounts the pain and trauma typically confronted by a doctor hit with a malpractice suit, or declares that the medical malpractice system should be reformed to rid the system of the truly bad and incompetent doctors who "give the medical profession a bad name," but that in doing so great care be taken not to "throw out the baby (i.e., the entire health care industry) with the bath water," he is immediately *believable*. And seemingly genuine! And, that is why, when author Rapp bemoans the role of certain class of plaintiffs' attorneys in instigating baseless medical malpractice lawsuits, or excessive court awards against doctors, or when he declares that the present system of court-based 'remedy' for the aggrieved patient, provides no real remedy for him, he, again, is immediately *believable*. And genuine!

THIS, in a word, is precisely why I wholeheartedly commend SO *YOU REALLY WANT TO SUE YOUR DOCTOR!* to every person or entity with any stake whatsoever in the subject matter of this book, or any with a genuine interest in it, as a highly competent, well balanced, objective 'must read' on the subject. Clearly, doctors, nurses, healthcare providers, hospital administrators, patients, lawyers, malpractice trial practitioners, medical practice policy makers, and just plain citizens, will find this book of great interest, value, and benefit, among many others.

Enjoy it! Thank you all.
Benjamin O. Anosike, Ph.D.
LAW BOOKS AUTHOR, EDITOR

1st PREFACE
By James W. Sutherland, M.D.

In *this* courageous and almost unique approach to the problem of malpractice in the United States of America today, Dr. Roy T. Rapp presents, in *SO YOU REALLY WANT TO SUE YOUR DOCTOR!*, a crystal clear overview of what is involved in practical, realistic terms in the 'real world' of medical practice, in a patient suing his or her doctor.

His primary purpose can be summed up in one word: *EDUCATION.* Simply put, he would like patients who ever gets tempted to do so, either because of a legitimate cause or primarily out of some outside pressures or inducement by malpractice trial lawyers or their advertisements, to ask themselves these vital questions. "Do I have a real claim?" "Do I realize how long and arduous the course could be upon which I am about to embark?" "Do I realize the potential wreckage and ruin that such action by me could bring to the lives of a physician and his/her family, and, more important, possibly to the very existence of the whole American health care delivery system, itself, which we all treasure so dearly?"

Most commendably but appropriately, is one of the most vital, relevant points which has needed constant emphasizing, even over and over and over again in the whole medical malpractice issue, but has hardly ever been communicated or otherwise imparted to the American public or the patient population by the malpractice trial lawyers and the professional champions of 'the right to sue.' That issue is appropriately lent the right emphasis that it well deserves in this book. Namely, the central truth that even a proof merely of a bad result or a medical mishap in a given case, is not necessarily evidence of lack of skill or negligence on the part of a physician in all cases. And should not automatically be viewed as that in a case!

Among many of its other strong points, are the legal chapters of the book. The chapters on approaching the attorney by a client, on pursuing the case, pre-trial skirmishes between the suing patient's attorney and the defending doctor's attorney, and the malpractice trial itself, are very clear and comprehensible (even to this lay observer). They are comprehensive, yet are simple. To the question thereafter, "Should some doctors be sued?" Dr. Rapp's answer is emphatic and unequivocal: *absolutely*! Not only that, Dr. Rapp goes further and contends that if the charge of bad doctoring leveled on a doctor shows a dangerous trend in the professional conduct of the given doctor, suspension of that doctor's license should be sought, but should be FIRST and FOREMOST, even before money is pursued by the plaintiff.

One subject of vital interest is the '*gridlock*' that is currently affecting medical practice and the delivery of health in the United States today. The reasons for this state of affairs, are obvious: access for some patients is difficult; cost is at times excessive; and in many instances the reality of unrealistic expectations for a total success or cure by patients, is a major factor which leads to suits against doctors.

In the words of Dr. Rapp, "A simplistic explanation of the core problem suggests that the system has become too sophisticated, too fragmented, and too expensive. New drugs, new techniques, new diagnostic tools, etc - all these are happening too fast for the economy to be able to absorb or digest it, or to pay."

Aside from published statistics and clear public records and documentation on it, as a physician in practice for several decades, myself, I personally know for sure just from real practical experience alone, if nothing else, that having a practice insurance policy has become progressively more and more expensive by the year these days. Is it any wonder that doctors, as well as patients, alike, today yearn for the 'good old days' of health care, when mothers had their babies at home, when doctors and their patients were (almost all) friends, and lawsuits were rare!?

Sadly, it looks as though this present gridlock will continue for a while. Dr. Rapp ends by proffering some reforms that would get to the root causes of the present problem, and offer a working alternative to the ongoing gridlock. Being freedom-loving Americans that we are, the vast majority of Americans, I can almost certainly wager, would not want to ever come to the point where they'll have no other choice other than the one which Dr. Rapp realistically fears may come about, unless the present problem is urgently addressed, "a national health care controlled by an ultimate dictator – the government." *The ultimate irony of this, is that in the final analysis, the American patients, themselves, will probably wind up losing the right to sue their doctors altogether for medical malpractice, irrespective of whether they like it or not. That is, UNLESS, of course, they rise up to do something about it NOW before it may become too late.*

What an excellent book that comes along at such a timely moment for America in the midst of a raging national debate for "tort reform," and what to do about the worsening problem of malpractice 'gridlock' in the health care delivery system today! My fellow physicians, as well as the malpractice trial attorneys, the patients, health care providers, and others, will surely benefit immensely from the treasure of pertinent information contained in this book.

James W. Sutherland., M.D., Ch.M. (Hons.) Glasgow, F.R.C.S. Eng. F.R.C.S.

2nd PREFACE

By James A. Rapp, J.D., Attorney-at-Law

Surveys of the professions that humans engaged in societies, always rank physicians at the top, or nearly the top, of the most respected professions in the world. Why, then, is there so much talk of suing doctors? The answer is actually quite simple. Success!

Attorneys (persons like me, of course!) are fond of pointing out that at the time during which the drafters were writing our Constitution, medicine practiced bloodletting - a treatment that led to the death of the Father of Our Country, George Washington. In the more than 200 years since its adoption, the U.S. Constitution has been amended only a few dozen times or so. However, it's worth noting that during this same very period, changes in medicine have been nothing short of revolutionary. We have gone from a nation with an average life expectancy of around 35 years when the Constitution was adopted, to one of nearly 80 years! What a big, big difference!

The road of the law has been paved with equality and justice (although just what that means has varied over our history). Advances in medicine have been forged with a mixture of quackery, gore, experimentation, accident, luck, death, science ... and many successes. Some of the greatest advances in medicine, ironically, have resulted during times of tragedy or war. With each advance, there were many other hoped-for cures or treatments of no avail. And that remains so today.

In our America, we are a country where we accept that some will be found guilty, and others innocent, in civil or criminal trials. We accept, when it comes to the arena of law, for example, that the legal system isn't perfect, but yet we accept and believe in it, nonetheless.

BUT, NOT QUITE SO, THOUGH, WHEN IT COMES TO THE ARENA OF MEDICINE AND THE DOCTOR! Quite simply, when it comes to our doctors, by contrast, we expect from them a remedy for every ache, every pain, ailment, illness, or disease whatsoever, whether it's occasioned from nature, some mishap, or even our own doing or self-neglect. We give doctors no room for human mistake or error. We can't accept that there might not quite be a cure for every problem. We have come to expect success in each and every single instance. And then when there isn't, we wonder whether the doctor is somehow to blame. "Should I sue the doctor?"

In this book, *SO YOU REALLY WANT TO SUE YOUR DOCTOR!*, Roy T. Rapp, M.D., invites readers to enter the real world of medical malpractice litigation, from beginning to its end. He brings the unique and special perspective that only a practicing and experienced physician can provide. He accepts that there are some doctors who should be sued and drummed out of the profession. He also recognizes that there are many other times when we expect a level of perfection - even miracles - that the medical professional simply cannot deliver. *SO YOU REALLY WANT TO SUE YOUR DOCTOR!* helps the readers know and appreciate the difference.

Dr. Rapp practices in his hometown, Quincy, Illinois, and has for a half century done so. He is a graduate of the University of Illinois Medical School in Chicago. After an internship/residency at Cook County Hospital and Illinois Research and Educational Hospital in Chicago, and a stint of military duty, he moved to the coal mining area along the West Virginia and Kentucky border, famed for the Hatfield-McCoy feud. He subsequently returned to his hometown, went through a general surgical residency at St. Francis Hospital in Peoria, and opened The Rapp Clinic. He has been board certified by the American Board of Abdominal Surgery and the American Board of Family Practice. Among other recognitions, in 2004 he was given a Lifetime Achievement Award by the Illinois Academy of Family Physicians, and a Distinguished Service Award for his many years of service in medical practice.

Author Roy T. Rapp has always maintained an interest in both the law and medicine. Of his six children - among whom I am one - four of them are practicing lawyers, and one, is a physician who is also a lawyer. This book painstakingly merges and integrates these two basic interests.

The city of Quincy, by coincidence, is the location of an early medical malpractice case. Dr. Ritchey was found negligent when he did not properly set a broken wrist. It was alleged that he had used the wrong size splints and did not put them in the proper place, resulting in the fracture failing to heal properly and causing the patient's hand to become deformed and disabled. Abraham Lincoln unsuccessfully represented Dr. Ritchey on appeal in 1860; in the same year, the Illinois Supreme Court upheld the judgment against Dr. Ritchey.

Medical malpractice litigation was complicated way back then in Dr. Richey's time; and remains so today. For patients, their families, and even doctors and lawyers, this book will provide a helpful, informative, and informed insight into what is really involved, both from the medical, legal and patient's perspectives, when you think about suing your doctor.

INTRODUCTION

THE BASIC PURPOSE OF THIS BOOK

- If the American health care is, by most expert accounts worldwide, the best in the world, why is it in a gridlock?
- Is it because, for many, access to such care is difficult and even impossible?
- Is it because the cost is often high or excessive?
- Is it because of the impersonal attitude of health care providers?
- Is it because of the often unrealistic, even utopian expectations of the patients?

Such factors have been offered by many analysts and commentators – patients or former patients, doctors, independent observers, etc – as the primary cause for the long-standing "crisis" in the American health care system. Nevertheless, whatever the actual causes, one thing is obvious and not disputed by many, if any at all, namely, that the system is in serious trouble.

In response to this, the government devotes an inordinate amount of time and resources to an illusionary quest for a solution. When no meaningful solution is apparent to patients in their own lives, they frequently express their dissatisfaction and frustrations by bringing medical malpractice suits against their doctors. These forays to the courthouses of America have not resolved the primary issue for the patient, however: IMPROVEMENT IN THE QUALITY OF HEALTHCARE FOR HIM OR HER. In fact, the major by product, has been that the resultant medical malpractice crisis has driven a wedge between the health care providers, on the one hand, and their patients, on the other hand. In consequence, an unfortunate but increasing phenomenon is that, today it is not uncommon to find that doctors regard almost every patient as a potential litigant, and try to shield themselves by practicing "defensive medicine," thus further exacerbating the problem even more for the average patient by escalating the cost of health care.

For most other people, there is life after a lawsuit. But not so for the physician, however! Even if in the end, after the grueling ordeal of a lawsuit, he prevails, the experience already makes an indelible imprint on him or her that forever affects his/her professional performance and can even cause the doctor to abandon a career that took twelve to sixteen years of his life in intensive and costly preparation.

Doctors, on their own part, bitterly complain that patients should understand that medicine is not an exact science. American patients, on the other hand, are not impressed by this argument; because, for the most part, they have been programmed by the popular culture to expect, virtually as though a citizenship 'entitlement,' the very latest state-of-the-art medical care with a perfect outcome. When this presumed entitlement does not seem readily forthcoming, they become angry and flock to the lawyers and the courts as their remedy because no other remedy is readily apparent, and the malpractice lawyers' media saturation advertisement makes the legal option seem all the more the only 'remedy' that's advisable or available.

1

Plaintiffs' (i.e., patients') attorneys who, of course, make a livelihood out of medical malpractice 'liability' and 'tort' law, would rather have the present tort system that provides only for substantial money awards as the only option. A few concerned patients would prefer licensure suspension and revocation for the bad or incompetent doctor who does professional wrong in order to rid the profession of "bad doctors." Nevertheless, their attorneys are quick to point out what, to them, is the 'folly' of such thinking. In the final analysis, then, the injured patient under the present tort system of medical malpractice, thereby remains largely uncompensated.

It must be stated, most emphatically, that most medical doctors are competent. Unfortunately, however, a few who are below average have squeezed into the profession. Part of the problem, according to many analysts and a common impression, is attributable to the perception, if not the reality, that medical schools no longer attract only the brightest and most altruistic. Furthermore, today, in this modern era, the perception is also widespread among many Americans that medicine has lost its luster and consequently the physician and his/her services are not adequately compensated or appreciated. These factors and others have converged to weaken a health delivery system that has the potential to be truly the best in the world.

Until, ultimately, effective corrective measures are taken, American patients will probably continue to consider health care as being delivered in a cold, uncaring manner, and to view the courts as their only recourse. If you are a patient, and you feel that your doctor is guilty of some kind of real medical malpractice in his or her treatment of you, and you are considering filing a lawsuit, then this book is for you. It will tell you what medical malpractice is and what it is not; and what it is really all about.

This book primarily contends that there are surely circumstances and instances involving the patients when physicians may, and should, be sued. But there are also circumstances and instances when they should not be sued. The tragedy, however, is that unfortunately patients usually don't understand the difference between such two situations. And medical malpractice attorneys, because they primarily look at this from a "business" standpoint, do not help the situation by way of helping the average patient see or make this differentiation. Rather, one of the very first things they'll often do in a case, will be to encourage the aggrieved patient to bring a suit even merely as a legal tactic or strategy in the hope simply of getting the doctor to offer a monetary settlement. Nor are they usually disappointed since the insurance companies would often find it cheaper to settle, than defend many claims.

The purpose of this book is to educate patients. For those with legitimate claims, it should make the process more understandable. For those with bogus claims, it should make the patient understand why the sued or threatened physicians are upset. In either case, the common hope and expectation is that this book will promote better discussions of the topic between the American physicians and the patients

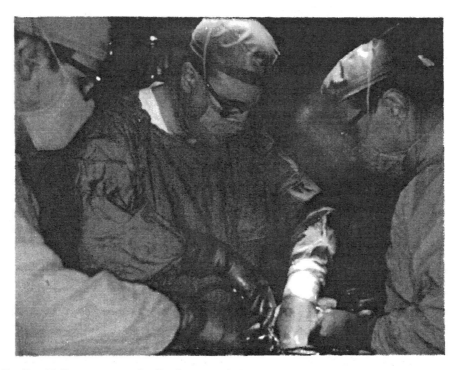

(1st Above) Dr. Roy T. Rapp, veteran family doctor and abdominal surgeon (center), operating, aided by Dr. Eric Shoengood, Assistant Surgeon (right), and Jack Brown, Surgical Technician (left)
Second, below, the Quincy Illinois' THE RAPP CLINIC.

The Battle For Tort Reform Is Raging On In America For Decades!

SPECIAL REPORT

A TALE OF TWO SYSTEMS

Western Europeans smoke, take Vioxx, and buy Firestone tires, too. But when they get injured claims are handled far differently. Here's a simplified summary of the key differences between their system and ours...

	EUROPE	U.S.
MEDICAL EXPENSES	National insurance plans cover most health costs.	Private coverage means more uninsured citizens and higher personal exposure.
EMOTIONAL AND PUNITIVE DAMAGES	Payments for emotional distress restricted. Punitives nonexistent.	Potential for lottery-like winnings for a small percentage of victims.
JURIES	Payment rulings made by administrative judges with fee schedules.	Justice is dispensed by ordinary citizens. No scientific or business expertise required.
CONTINGENT FEES	Qu'est-ce que c'est?	Plaintiffs' lawyers rake in 33% to 40% of their clients' winnings.

... and how they play out for all involved

	EUROPE	U.S.
SIZE OF AWARDS	Much smaller. Even extreme emotional distress does not lead to larger awards.	Much bigger. Thanks to sympathetic juries, multimillion-dollar verdicts common.
SPEED OF PAYMENT	Faster. No adversarial process. Less room for pretrial maneuvering or appeals.	Slower. It can take years for victims to recover their money.
LAWYER POPULATION	Much smaller. Very few call themselves plaintiffs' attorneys.	More than 1 million, some 10% to 15% of whom represent plaintiffs.
PUBLICITY	Less elaborate pretrial discovery equals fewer smoking guns.	Battles that should be won in court are won in press—but public learns more.

FRENCH JUSTICE Juries don't hear injury cases

Doctors rally in Chicago, Illinois, for tort reform (Courtesy, Business Week's Special Report, "How To Fix The Tort Reform System," March 14, 2005)

CHAPTER I

A FEW 'HORROR STORIES' OF EXTREME OR CLEAR-CUT MEDICAL MALPRACTICE SITUATIONS THAT'LL ALMOST CERTAINLY PROMPT A MALPRACTICE LAWSUIT

Thirty five-year-old **MARY SMITH**, a patient, entered an above average general hospital for treatment. Her urologist had told her that her left kidney was diseased and needed to be removed.

Mary was taken to surgery, and one of her kidneys was removed. But not the left kidney which was the 'diseased' one! Instead, it was her 'normal' right kidney that had been removed.

The doctor blamed this unfortunate misadventure on the operating room nurses as he claimed that they (the nurses) had placed the patient "wrong side up" on the operating table. But the nurses (the hospital) contended that it was the duty of the operating surgeon to be certain that it was the proper organ that he was removing.

In the eyes of the law, this would be considered a *"res ipsa malpractice case"* (the lawyers jargon for a case which speaks for itself), and the patient would be almost automatically and certainly entitled to a huge monetary award. This was not what happened in this particular instance, though. Rather, the patient was never told straight out that the "wrong" kidney had inadvertently been removed, nor did the hospital record reveal the "mistake" and the fact that all she had left in her body was a "diseased" kidney in that it was the lone "normal" kidney she had that had been removed. Which would mean, for her, that she would need the medical treatment of dialysis, or even a complete kidney transplant, and that her life would be significantly shortened. The patient's health insurer, not having been informed or aware of this tragic medical mistake that had been made, paid the patient's bill and the patient was discharged from the hospital.

In any modern hospital in operation today that's fully approved by the Joint Commission on Accreditation of Health Care Organizations, such a scenario is not supposed to happen, and if it does, at the very minimum, not only must the patient be timely and fully informed of it, but so also must the entire staff so that appropriate remedial action can be taken to avoid the future repetition of such a tragedy. This did not happen in this given instance in this duly approved American hospital, and it would be difficult to follow the paper trail and reconstruct the unfortunate event.

In another case in another Accredited American hospital, there was no cover-up or a serious injury of the kind described above to the patient in this instance. But there was a misdeed of a different sort. What was involved was an unjustified hospital bill.

In this case, the patient was hospitalized for treatment for severe congestive heart failure. In the process, he was inadvertently given, intravenously, two units of packed red blood cells that were intended for another patient. Overloading this patient's vascular system could have killed him. But, fortunately, this did not happen immediately, but the patient did die soon thereafter. The patient's physician did inform him of the incident and explained that the error was due to a laboratory/nursing mix-up by hospital employees. What actually triggered the anger and complaint of the patient's family was that, upon discharge from the hospital, his bill included the charge for the unnecessary two units of packed red cells!

Generally, when "horror" stories such as the above-mentioned come to light, patients are angry, they feel that they have been duped, and would frequently seek recompense in the courthouses. For example, a middle-aged woman was awarded the sum of 5.1 million dollars because she suffered a paralyzing stroke after being "misdiagnosed" as having the "flu." In another case, the parents of a newborn infant were awarded some 4.25 million dollars in a malpractice settlement because the obstetrician, during delivery, had physically handicapped and brain damaged the child permanently. In yet another instance, a physician settled, for one million dollars, a "wrongful death" claim brought by the family of a 65-year-old man for alleged "inappropriate" treatment of an infection following brain surgery. And then, in another case, an amount of two million dollars was awarded to a 55-year-old plaintiff for having a stroke after being "misdiagnosed" as suffering from "depression and arthritis."

The portrait is not particularly appetizing for either the medical professionals or their patients. It is one of two opposing forces or gladiators facing each other in the battlefield – the patients on the one hand, are in serious need of care, but are distrustful of the delivery system; yet they are forced to entrust such care, even their very lives, to physicians and nurses who, on the other hand, are spooked by the constant threat of malpractice suits by the same patients. Clearly, the resulting standoff from such confrontation does not bode well for the American health care system!

HERE'S THE CENTRAL POINT HERE. It is, simply, most unfortunately, one overarching medical reality of today in America, is that unfortunately the courts have become the forum for resolving medical or health-related dissatisfactions as well as disagreements among Americans. And, consequently, if you, the patient, ever come to the point where you've become convinced that your doctor or other health care provider has committed an act of medical malpractice against you, and you are unable to resolve your differences with your health care providers in any other way other than to sue, you should read this book. *It will tell you when and how to do it – the appropriate situations when you should, as well as the right ways to do it. And, just as importantly, how and when not to.*

6

CHAPTER II

WHAT CONSTITUTES A TRUE MEDICAL MALPRACTICE ACT IN LAW?

A. NEGLIGENCE IS THE DOMINANT THEORY OF LIABILITY IN MEDICAL MALPRACTICE

Generally, in medical malpractice litigation, the predominant theory of liability is "negligence." In order to recover for a negligence-based malpractice (negligent malpractice), the plaintiff (i.e., you, the patient) must establish the following elements:

1. the existence of the physician's duty to the plaintiff, usually based upon the existence of the physician-patient relationship;
2. the applicable standard of care and the violation of that standard;
3. a compensable injury; and
4. a causal connection between the violation of that standard of care and the harm that's complained of.

B. MALPRACTICE JUDICIALLY DEFINED

At the end of a jury trial, the judge instructs the jury as to the legal elements which constitute 'medical malpractice' under the law. One such instruction under the State of Illinois law defines malpractice as follows:

MALPRACTICE

Duty of Physician, Surgeon, Dentist

in (treating) (operating upon) a patient, a (doctor/dentist) must possess and apply the knowledge and use the skill and care that is ordinarily used by reasonably well qualified (doctors/dentists) in the locality in which he practices or in similar localities' cases or circumstances. A failure to do so is a form of negligence that is called malpractice. (The only way in which you may decide whether the defendant possessed and applied the knowledge, and used the skill and care, which the law required of him, is from evidence presented in this trial by (doctors/dentists) called as expert witnesses. You must not attempt to determine this question from any personal knowledge you have).

HERE'S A CENTRAL POINT TO REMEMBER: When you are considering filing a medical malpractice suit against your doctor, clearly bear in mind that the fact that there's been a bad result from your doctor's work at the end of a medical treatment or procedure, or even a bad mistake on his part, is not necessarily or automatically a medical malpractice.

Just because you are angry at your doctor, or because he had sued or threatened to sue you for a bill, does not mean that you can run to court and make wild accusations that can ultimately stick as real medical malpractice. For it to constitute real medical malpractice, such deed or action by your doctor, or other health care provider, must have violated the statutes (the actual laws) of your state in regard to medical malpractice.

C. THE TORT LAW

Medical malpractice law is generally based, at the outset, on traditional tort law principles. Alternative theories, such as breach of contract, are seldom charged. Broadly speaking, a 'tort' is a civil or private wrong, other than breach of a contract, for which a court will provide a remedy in the form of an action for damages. (1)

Unlike criminal law, which is concerned with the protection of interests common to the public at large, often exacting a penalty from the wrongdoer, tort law is directed toward the compensation of individuals, rather than the public, for losses that they might have suffered.

D. NEGLIGENCE THEORY OF TORT LIABILITY

Generally: There are various theories of tort liability. As stated earlier in this chapter, in medical malpractice cases, "negligence" is generally the applicable tort theory. Unlike an intentional tort, such an assault, negligence may be based on omissions or failures to act. (3) Of course, under some unusual circumstances, a physician may be liable for an intentional tort. In those instances, the physician usually can be sued not only for money damages, but also be prosecuted for a criminal offense. In the typical case, however, the physician is sued only for money damages. There may be some solace in this distinction for the physician because although he can lose everything that he could possibly earn in a lifetime as a result of a single adverse medical malpractice verdict, he will not be sentenced to jail or even executed unless he is convicted for the offense under the criminal law!

Elements of Medical Malpractice
A doctor's negligence in medical malpractice requires that four basic elements be established:
Duty: The treating physician must have incurred a duty to care for the patient – a physician-patient relationship must exist.

Breach of Standard of Care: The physician must have failed to perform, or must have breached, that duty by deviating from the standard of care in his community. This is the 'negligence' aspect. With a few exceptions, the standard of care must be established by the expert testimony of other health providers.

Injury: The patient himself or herself must be injured or damaged.

Proximate Cause: The negligence of the physician must be the 'proximate cause' of the injury or damage claimed.

1. Duty: Physician-Patient Relationship

The obligation of a physician to care for a patient primarily arises by virtue of the physician-patient relationship. A physician ordinarily does not have a duty or obligation to accept or to treat a patient even though that patient may be seriously ill and in danger of dying. However, once the physician accepts the patient, a physician-patient relationship is automatically established between them and thereafter he now has the duty to use the kind of skill and care consistent with the standard of care required and expected by law in caring for that patient.

2. The Standard of Care

The Appropriate Standard of Care expected has traditionally been determined by comparing a physician's care of a patient with that customarily rendered by physicians in the same community. This is known as the "locality rule." The notion that a physician should be held to the standard of care existing in the physician's own community was developed by the American courts in the 19th century to protect the rural physician, who was presumed to have possessed less education and less access to adequate facilities and equipment than a physician practicing in a large urban area. (4)

The "locality rule" has been attacked by some attorneys as being outmoded for a number of reasons. First, it is said, the application of the rule in a strict fashion could act to deny an injured patient's recovery where his treatment was clearly negligent even though consistent with the practices prevailing in his own community. (5). In other words, says the argument, this may mean that the medical profession as a whole may be negligent. Second, it is said that a "conspiracy of silence" among physicians in a community could deny a patient an expert medical testimony that is necessary to his case. (6) In other words, that physicians won't tell if another physician is negligent. Third, attorneys point out that limitations on travel or opportunities for continuing education, which used to be a real factor in the past, no longer exist in today's environment.

Largely because of such criticisms of the locality rule, the patients' attorneys today often prefer to hold every physician, regardless of the area or facility where he practices, to a national standard. In other words, by and large today a small-town physician would be expected to exercise the same care as the most proficient physician who's practicing in a huge metropolitan center.

Nevertheless, although some States have abandoned the locality rule, most have not. Instead, the model employed is that a physician's conduct is to be judged by the standard of care of a reasonably competent physician practicing in the same or similar community. Thus, a national standard is not applied in a state like Illinois, for example. (7) Nevertheless, the term "locality" has no precise meaning and varies with the facts of each case considering the purposes of the rule (i.e., difference in continuing education opportunities, lack of medical research centers available to rural practitioners, and transportation difficulties.) (8)

Even where the locality rule is used, it is important to recognize that the patients' attorneys are constantly trying to hack away at the rule (9) and eventually may convince a court to change it. Therefore, to be on the safe side, doctors gear their practice, to the extent at all possible, to conform to a national standard, but at the same time when faced with a malpractice suit, small town practitioners are cautioned never to let a patient's attorney trap them into suggesting that they are as good as the most eminent metropolitan practitioner. Attorneys may try to use this ploy to establish the right standard of care that will apply to your doctor whom you are accusing of malpractice.

When your case comes to the stage when it is presented to a jury, the court (judge) will usually summarize the "locality rule" to the jurors. An example will be this: (10)

In (treating) (operating upon) a patient, a (doctor) (dentist) must possess and apply the knowledge and use the skill and care that is ordinarily used by reasonably well qualified (doctors) (dentists) in the locality in which he practices or in similar localities in similar cases or circumstances. A failure to do so is a form of negligence that is called malpractice. (11)

A physician who holds himself out as a specialist in a particular branch of medicine is also subject to a "locality rule," but must use the skill and care, which reasonably well-qualified specialists practicing in the same branch of medicine have and use.

A court summarizes the "locality rule," as it applies to specialists, as follows:
In (treating) (operating upon) a patient, a (doctor) (dentist) who holds himself out as a specialist and undertakes service in a particular branch of medical, surgical, or other healing science, must possess and apply the knowledge and use the skill and care which reasonable well-qualified specialists in the same field, practicing in the same locality, or in similar localities and circumstances use. A failure to do so is a form of negligence that is called malpractice. (12)

To establish the standard of care that applies in the case of your doctor, your attorney would almost certainly have to present expert testimony. In deed, he would have to do so UNLESS the malpractice charged is obvious, as in a documented case where a sponge is left in the abdomen. (13) The expert must, of course, testify as to what exactly the standard of care is that is required in the same or a similar locality in which the physician accused of malpractice practices.

Equally important, the testifying expert must also be of the same "school of medicine" as the allegedly negligent physician. The law recognizes the different schools of medicine and does not favor one over another. It reasons that since the different schools have differing methods of treatment and practice, it would be inequitable to have the conduct of a duly licensed practitioner of one school judged by the standards of a different school of medicine.

Breach of Duty: Theories of Liability

If a physician has a duty to you, he will be deemed to be negligent if he violates or breaches that duty. Attorneys describe violations of a physician's duty by various theories of liability or causes of action. Basically, these (the causes of action) denote the forms that medical malpractice may take. Such causes of action are discussed in detail in the next chapter.

Once again, let us emphasize that as an aggrieved patient of a doctor or hospital, when considering whether there is a breach of duty by a doctor (or hospital), it is important to recognize that merely proving that a good result was not achieved is not proof of a breach of your doctor's duty. Instead, your attorney must have to demonstrate what the average, reasonable physician in good standing would have done in a similar case. Proof of a bad result or a mishap is simply no evidence of lack of skill or negligence. Another way of putting across the point, is this: If your physician has given you the benefit of his best judgment, assuming that judgment to be equal to that ordinarily used by reasonably well-qualified physicians in similar cases, he is not liable for negligence, even if that judgment is erroneous. (14)

3.   Damages: Injury

Assuming that you have indeed been injured through a physician's negligence, then you must also incur damages. Damages are compensated by money to pay you for the losses suffered. There are several types of damages. General categories include the following:

Special damages are those damages that directly resulted from the negligence. For example, if a surgeon leaves an instrument in a patient, the patient will incur the costs of having another operation to remove the instrument. The cost of that additional operation is 'special' damage.

General damages are those damages, which more generally result from the negligence. For example, it generally follows that the patient having a surgical instrument removed in a second operation will incur some additional pain and suffering as a result. That pain and suffering is a 'general' damage.

Punitive or exemplary damages are damages designed to punish a person sued. They are commonly awarded in cases of intentional torts. They are seldom awarded in medical malpractice cases.

4. Causation: Proximate Cause

Next, it is not enough for you to show that your doctor was negligent, or that you actually incurred some injuries or damages from that. In addition, you must also be able to establish that your doctor's negligence caused your injuries. If your doctor's treatment did not cause injury, or the lack of treatment did not affect the result, then your doctor is not liable.

Summary: Negligence Theory of Tort Liability

To summarize, in order to be able to recover in a medical malpractice case, you must, generally by the use of expert testimony, establish or prove the following: (15)

1. *Duty* – that your doctor had a duty to care for you.

2. *Negligence* – that your doctor was negligent and did not meet the standard of care used in your community.

3. *Injury* –That you sustained some injury or damages by reason of your doctor's negligence.

4. *Proximate Cause* – That your doctor's action (or inaction) was the cause of your injury.

Breach of Contract

Medical malpractice claims are most often brought in the context of tort law. However, a contract theory is sometimes, though infrequently, raised. Under this theory, you may argue that your doctor had a contract to care for you for which you paid the consideration by way of a fee. And that by failing to competently care for you, your doctor has violated or breached that contract. And for that reason, you are seeking damages. Because damages are normally more limited under contract law than tort law, breach of contract claims are usually raised, however, merely as an additional or alternative theory of relief.

CHAPTER III

THE MAIN REASONS FOR WHICH PHYSICIANS GET SUED

According to the insurance company statistics, physicians are usually sued because:

- Because a physician failed to properly diagnose the patient.
  These cases most often involve misdiagnosis of cancer, a fracture or dislocation, abdominal problems, a heart problem or an infection.

- Because a physician failed to properly treat the patient.
  Mistreatment frequently involving childbirth cases, drug effects or selection, infection and fractures or dislocations.

- Because of a surgical complication that occurs.
  These cases often involve post-operative complications, inadvertent or inappropriate procedures, or delays in performing surgery.

The Acceptable 'Causes Of Action' That Apply In Medical Malpractice

In formal terms, among malpractice lawyers circumstances that may give rise to malpractice claim are referred to as *"causes of action."* Put very simply, the courts have simply established the CAUSES OF ACTION that any charge or accusation of malpractice you make against your doctor must fit into. And while it is, of course, possible for your attorney to propose other causes of action beyond these usual ones, the courts are generally reluctant to plow up new law.

The following are the acceptable CAUSES OF ACTION that generally apply in medical malpractice.

1. CONSENT: There must be the Proper and Informed Consent
Except in an emergency situation, an adult person may not be "touched" by a doctor without his or her permission. If your doctor violates this prohibition, you may be able to sue for assault and battery.

A.   Battery: The General Consent Requirement
A physician has a duty not to touch or have contact with you, such as through surgical procedure, without your consent. And a physician, who touches or has contact with a patient without such consent by the patient, has committed battery.
The offenses of 'assault' and of 'battery' are often expressed as twin torts. However, in real terms a doctor is very seldom accused of committing assault in connection with his medical practice. Technically, in the context of the law, assault ordinarily refers to the apprehension of touching or contact felt by the "victim"; battery, on the other hand, refers to the touching or contact itself. To establish that he (she) is a victim of battery, a patient need not establish that the doctor intended harm. In fact, the doctor may have actually

helped the patient. The basis of the action is merely the failure on the doctor's part to have obtained the patient's consent.

EXAMPLE: Parmella Davis had been admitted to a sanatorium for treatment of epilepsy. After examination, it was determined that her uterus was contracted and lacerated and that the lower portion of her rectum was diseased. She was operated upon for these difficulties. After this initial surgery, she returned to her home, but several weeks later was again taken to the sanatorium for a second operation during which her ovaries and uterus were removed. Although Mrs. Davis had consented to the first operation, she did not consent to the removal of any organs. In consequence, the Illinois Supreme Court found, in the case involving the above scenario, that the physician was liable for damages by removing the organs without the patient's consent. (1)

The required consent may be given in several ways:

B.   Oral Consent. This is your expressed consent given verbally and not in writing. It is common in non-surgical situations. You may say, "Doctor, will you check my blood pressure?" Or, your doctor may say, "Let me take your blood pressure," with you responding, "fine."

C.   Written Consent. This is your expressed consent but given in writing. It is common in surgical situations or when other than routine treatment is provided. With the development of the informed consent doctrine, written consents have become particularly common. Hospitals routinely require written consent on admission.

D.   Implied or Assumed Consent. This is a consent which is not expressed, but is presumed to exist by virtue of the circumstances or your actions. EXAMPLE: A doctor may say to you, "I would like to examine your shoulder," and you remove your shirt without saying a word. Under this circumstance, it is said to be 'implied' or assumed that you have consented to the examination. Similarly, if you appear at a doctor's office complaining of a sore throat, you are requesting diagnosis and treatment. The doctor may touch you, do appropriate laboratory tests and, in his best judgment, give appropriate medication, both oral and intramuscular. His consent is 'implied' or assumed if you do not object to what is being done.

A patient's consent is not required when an emergency exists, either before or during treatment or surgery. In such circumstances, the law effectively presumes that the patient would, if able, consent to the treatment or surgery. When a case is presented to a jury, the court (the judge) will usually summarize the emergency exception in the case of surgery, for example, in the following language:

Ordinarily, a [surgeon] must obtain the consent of a patient before operating on him. However, if an emergency arises that requires treatment in order to protect the patient's health and it is impossible or impracticable to obtain consent either from the patient or someone authorized to consent for him, a [surgeon] may undertake treatment, provided that what he does is within the customary practice of reasonably well-qualified [surgeons] practicing in the same or similar localities in similar cases and circumstances. (2)

E.   Informed Consent. A physician has a duty or obligation to inform his patient in ordinary, understandable language, of the nature of the patient's ailment or condition, the risks and results of any alternative methods of treatment, including failing to undergo any treatment at all, so that the patient himself can make an informed and intelligent decision on whether to submit to a proposed course of treatment or surgical procedure. (3) Doctors are reminded that when seeking a consent, the patient should always be given the opportunity to ask questions and that an informed consent should be obtained prior to providing treatment.

The requirement of an informed consent developed from battery cases. Initially, for example, courts would find that a battery occurred although there was "consent" if that consent was given prior to being informed by the doctor of the risks involved in treatment and surgery. Beginning around 1960, however, it began to be recognized that the matter was really one of the standards of professional conduct, and so negligence and the informed consent doctrine generally displaced battery as the basis for liability. (4)

Attorneys generally discount the charge of lack of informed consent as grounds of malpractice whenever and if it could at least be assumed or established that there was some consent at all. This stems from the fact that in a state like Illinois, for example, expert medical testimony must be presented to establish what should be explained to a patient when lack of informed consent is claimed. (5) A doctor has only a duty to disclose those risks, results or alternatives that a reasonable medical practitioner of the same school, in the same or similar circumstances, would have disclosed. (6) Further, a doctor is not required to disclose every conceivable risk which possibly could develop, but only those factors which, either alone or in combination with other factors, which the patient would view as significant enough as to influence a patient's decision of whether to consent to treatment or surgery. (7) As wisely recognized by one court:

This [doctor-patient relationship] not only vests the doctor with the responsibility of disclosure, but also requires the doctor to exercise discretion in prudently disclosing information in accordance with his patient's best interests. To disclose more than that which is material would run counter to the responsibility assumed through the doctor-patient relationship. (8)

Thus, it is accepted that excessive disclosure of remote risks would tend to do more harm than good to the patient. A doctor is obligated only to disclose common risks reasonably known that may result from the proposed treatment or surgery. Clearly, risks of death and serious bodily harm or disfigurement should be disclosed.

As in the case of battery, informed consent is not required where a patient is incompetent or mentally or physically unable to provide his consent and treatment is immediately necessary. Further, a patient may well decline to listen to a detailed list of possible complications.

According to one sociologist, medical patients "are more often bullied than informed into consent." (9) It is important to remember, however, that an adult, competent patient has the right to refuse treatment or surgery even if that refusal is tantamount to personal suicide. It has been suggested that there is something almost natural about a sick patient deferring to the wishes of his doctor. (10) Defensively, a doctor must make certain that the decision whether to receive treatment or surgery is the patient's, not the doctor's.

F.   Consent for or by Minors. Except in a case of emergency treatment or first aid, the physician who conducts the examination or treatment, including surgery, of a minor, has the duty to obtain the consent of the child's parent or legal guardian. (11) A "minor" is a person who, because of his age, is considered to be legally incompetent or unable to enter into legal agreements or relationships. A minor generally may not, for example, consent to medical treatment or surgery. In Illinois, as in most states in the United States, the general legal age or age of majority is 18 years of age. (12) A person 18 years of age is legally competent and may, accordingly, consent to medical treatment or surgery. (1)

Under certain circumstances, the law extends legal competency to minors. This has happened in the case of medical care. Thus, for example, a person may usually consent to a medical treatment or surgery on his own, although he/she is a minor, if married or pregnant. (14) In addition, state laws may allow a minor to consent to treatment in other circumstances. A common example involves birth control.

Where a minor is unable to consent to treatment or surgery, the consent of his parent or legal guardian is required. Indeed, even where a minor can consent, it is still generally advisable to obtain the consent of a parent or legal guardian providing the child's treatment would not thereby be jeopardized.

Parents are the natural custodians and guardians of their children. (15) As such, a parent generally has authority to consent to his child's treatment or surgery. A parent even has authority to consent to treatment or surgery although himself is a minor. (16)

If the parents are divorced, the custody of a child may be placed with either or both parents. Where custody is granted to one parent, that parent has total control of a child's health care unless the parents otherwise agree or the court granting the divorce (17) otherwise directs. (18) Where a joint custody is granted, the parents are to agree or the court is to determine the rights and responsibilities of the parents for the physical care, including health care, of the child. (19) Unfortunately, many agreements and court determinations are prone to being vague, or simply state that these decisions will be made "jointly." Where the parents are divorced, the physicians and hospitals may require the consent of both parents to a child's medical care, particularly in non-emergency situations, unless the authority of one parent is clear.

Where parents are unfit, a court may appoint a legal guardian. There are actually two types of legal guardians – a guardian of a child's estate and a guardian of a child's person. This may be the same person, but may be different. A guardian of a child's estate is in charge of his "estate," that is, his money and assets. (20) A guardian of a child's person is in charge of his custody, nurture and education. (21) It is the GUARDIAN of a child's person who must consent to medical treatment or surgery, but the GUARDIAN of the child's estate that must pay for it. The courts provide the legal guardians with "Letters of Office" or papers to prove their authority.

The consent of a minor's parent or legal guardian need not be obtained where a hospital, doctor or dentist renders emergency treatment, or first aid or care, if obtaining such a consent is not reasonably feasible under the circumstances without adversely affecting the condition of the minor's health. (22)

16

Because the consent of the minor's parents is generally required prior to treating the minors, a parent may decline to allow his child to receive health care. Religious beliefs may, for example, interfere with what is considered the proper diagnosis and treatment. Jehovah's Witnesses prohibit the transfusion of blood and Christian Scientists rely on prayer as the only therapy for disease. When a doctor or hospital believes that an accepted life-saving treatment is being withheld by a parent or guardian, the doctor or hospital will usually contact the area's Prosecuting Attorney for the county in which the child resides. Under certain circumstances, a minor may be considered a "neglected" person if the child is not provided the necessary medical care, and a court may then order that the appropriate medical care be provided, or appoint a legal guardian with the authority to consent to the minor's medical care.

G.   Unauthorized Postmortem Procedures   In most states in the United States of America, the practice is that a physician may not perform postmortem procedures, including autopsies, or accept organ donations, without proper consent. This system differs somewhat with that followed in many other countries, however. In one European country, for an example, the applicable law is that if the attending doctor is not sure of the cause of death in a given case, an unlimited autopsy can be performed without the permission of the next of kin. This provides, in practice, unlimited fresh bodies on which visiting doctors can perform operations they witnessed in the surgical theater shortly before. In addition, organs, normal and pathological, can be retained and warehoused.

Most American doctors would probably concede outright that such a system would not receive enthusiastic support in the United States. Indeed, efforts to establish formal systems for organ donations in the United States have often been perceived as coercive and even ghoulish activities by the country's medical profession. Here in this country (and elsewhere, as well), the next-of-kin of a deceased person are generally said to have a primary interest in his or her body. While this is not a property right in a dead body in the ordinary sense, a right of possession of a decedent's remains devolves upon the next-of-kin in order to make possible its appropriate disposition thereof, whether by burial or otherwise. (23) In reality, however, the law primarily protects, and thereby expects the doctors and others to respect, the feelings of the survivors. (24) And when and where these feelings are not respected, the doctor may be sued for infliction of mental or emotional distress upon the survivors. (25) To address this problem of making sure that the necessary consent is obtained, most States have enacted statutes which provide that an autopsy may be performed only upon the authorization of one of the next-of-kin. (26)

Previously, the Joint Commission on Accreditation of Healthcare Organizations, which is the body that accredits hospitals, had specified that a certain percentage of autopsies shall have been performed by a hospital as a requirement for approval. That standard has now been largely abandoned, however. The current procedures today, is that if one of one's relatives dies, and even if there is no question of this being a coroner's case but the attending doctor thinks that an autopsy would serve a useful purpose, then he should sit down with the next-of-kin and explain all the details of the case, and then request permission of them for an autopsy. He must, of course, explain to them the reasons why having the autopsy is necessary, and inform them as well that this will be done at no charge, among other information. (For you, the decedent's surviving next-of-kin, please note that under no circumstances are you to agree to pay anything for this procedure, as this is almost always supposed to be done free of any charge to you).

However, if you should suspect or have any reason to suspect that malpractice has occurred in the case, or you are generally not satisfied with the treatment, here's what you (a decedent's next-of-kin) must first do. You should insist that an autopsy be performed – even if you have to pay for it. An autopsy may well turn out to be "the smoking gun evidence" that you need in order to be able to prove medical surgical malpractice. Here's the simple reality of the matter: instead of expressing your suspicions that medical malpractice might have occurred, in legal terms it is infinitely better if you were to quietly notify the attending doctor immediately after the decedent's death that the family wants an autopsy to find out what dear old dad had died from and to determine if he had any medical conditions that other members of the family might also have. (NOTE: Be sure to hurry and immediately notify the mortician of your wish to have this done BEFORE all the blood in the decedent's body would have been removed and the decedent is pumped full of chemicals which interfere with toxicology examinations and evidence of drug overdose.)

If you suspect a misadventure and your doctor stalls on ordering an autopsy, it's advisable that you go immediately to the County coroner, express your concerns to him and request (in writing) that he order an autopsy, but at a hospital other than where your relative was treated and died. In fact, as a rule, particularly in hospitals connected with a medical school (teaching institutions), it is the doctors themselves who are usually anxious to have you grant your permission for an autopsy to be done on a decedent, and it is usually the family that refuses to grant such permission. If you were to have a situation where you find the doctor reluctant to accede to your autopsy request, sometimes it might be due to a matter as simple and uncomplicated as having in the particular case a doctor (or doctors) who is of the unfeeling type, or one not concerned enough about going to the hospital to pronounce the patient dead and to console the family, but would rather depend on a nurse to perform those tasks for the doctor.

H.   Consents Concerning Organ Donations of Deceased Persons Of popular interest, is the issue of ORGAN DONATIONS. As in the case of autopsies, organ donations should not be made without the proper consent. Virtually all states have adopted the Uniform Anatomical Gift Act. (27) Under this Act, any competent adult, or certain designated relatives and persons, may give all or any part of a person's body for the purpose of education, research, therapy or transplantation. (28) *Such persons, and the order by which anatomical gifts may be made, are as follows:*

The Spouse,
Adult sons or daughters.
Either parent.

A guardian of the person of the decedent at the time of his death, and finally, any person authorized or under obligation to dispose of the body. (29)

The manner for making anatomical gifts is specified by the Act. During his   lifetime, a person may make a gift by Will or other signed document, such as an organ donation card, on a Driver's License. (30) Relatives may give permission by a signed document or by telegraphic, recorded telephonic, or other recorded message. (31)

Anatomical gifts are subject to revocation. (32) Additionally, if the institution or person to whom the gift is made has actual notice that the decedent no longer intended to make the gift, or that a relative of the class (e.g., adult sons or daughters) who have the right the gift oppose it, then the gift may not be accepted. (33)

The time of death of a person under the Act must be determined by a doctor who attends the person at death, or, if none, the doctor who certifies the death. However, doctor may not participate in the removal or transplantation of the part. (34) A doctor who in good faith follows the Act is not liable for any claim against him, civil or criminal. (35) What is important, in most postmortem cases, is that your doctor should be respectful and sensitive to the decedent's family.

2. DIAGNOSIS

Another Cause of Action for medical malpractice suit is diagnosis.

A.   Delayed Diagnosis
A physician has an obligation not to delay in making a definitive diagnosis. The need for defensive medicine is never as great as when making a diagnosis. Doctors have noted that if their son injures his ankle and an examination indicates a sprain, they would not order or recommend an immediate x-ray for the son's ankle right away. This is because, they say, even if the pain to the son were to persist and a fracture is revealed, such delay in a definitive diagnosis and treatment would really have no effect on the outcome. But, suppose, on the other hand, the injured person were a different person altogether, in fact, say a hostile patient. THE OBVIOUS CONSEQUENCE? Clearly, woe onto the doctor if that same protocol is followed with that hostile patient! For, almost certainly, his/her attorney would probably argue that the delay had in fact harmed the patient by resulting in pain, suffering, mental anguish and even loss of earnings and employment during the delay! (36)

Delayed diagnosis cases are most often based on a doctor's failure to have performed a proper patient examination or to have obtained appropriate tests. Here, the physicians are between the horns of dilemma. On one side, the principle of 'defensive medicine' requires the employment of ample examination and testing. On the other, medical insurers, and particularly the government Medicare and Medicaid programs, demand that examination and testing be kept at a minimum in order to minimize medical costs. Unfortunately for the doctors, when the doctors involved in a case are sued, however, no one ever points out or mentions that they saved the insurer or patient some money, hence the common practice is have the appropriate tests performed, any way, regardless of the cost or payment arrangements.

B.   Misdiagnosis
A physician has an obligation to diagnose those conditions and ailments which a physician with the appropriate skill and care would ordinarily diagnose under similar circumstances. An increasingly common form of medical malpractice claim is "misdiagnosis." Misdiagnosis may be claimed either because of a failure to diagnose a particular condition or because of simply missing it altogether. These claims are especially common in the area of cancer diagnosis.

Family practitioners, obstetricians, and emergency room doctors, are particularly vulnerable to this form of medical malpractice. Family practitioners see a wide variety of patients. Obstetricians are frequently accused of failing to recognize or anticipate a complication and taking appropriate action. Emergency room doctors, faced with patients who are often strangers and pressured from all sides to keep patients out of the hospital, are constantly in danger of missing a diagnosis.

Where a diagnosis is not clear, a doctor should refer the patient to another doctor or specialist for consultation. This has the advantage of promptly confirming or correcting a diagnosis.

3. TREATMENT

Another Cause of Action in medical malpractice is in the area of TREATMENT.

A.   Delayed Treatment

A physician has an obligation not to delay in providing the appropriate treatment. Closely related to claims of medical malpractice for delayed diagnosis, are claims which contend that the treatment was negligently delayed. Physicians, in effect, walk a fine line between over-treating and under-treating.

EXAMPLE: Terri Jones became pregnant in January at the age of 18. She consulted a physician in mid-July and a potential problem resulting from a below normal size pelvic area was noted. A pelvimetry exam was made on her, which indicated that it would be very risky for the baby to pass through the delivery canal in a normal fashion. The physician ultimately indicated that a Caesarean section was a possibility because of Terri's pelvic size and the fact that the baby was above average in size. No glucose tolerance test to determine diabetes, a condition often associated with larger babies, nor an ultrasound test, which would have indicated the size of the baby, were utilized.

Almost four weeks past the expected delivery date, Terri admitted herself to the hospital. The staff was not alerted to schedule a Caesarean section and continuous fetal monitoring was not ordered. After examining Terri around 8:30 a.m., the physician left the hospital but checked several times as to her progress. At approximately noon, the doctor returned. The baby's heart tones had begun to drop and the baby was in distress. No Caesarean section was ordered, as the physician believed that there was not sufficient time left. At 12:16 p.m., a prolapsed cord was noted. (37) The physician attempted to push the baby back up the birth canal and off the cord. He was unsuccessful, as the baby, being too large for the mother's pelvis, was stuck. An attempt was then made to remove the baby from the womb through the use of forceps, but this was unsuccessful. The last heartbeat of the fetus was noted as 12:35 p.m. Also, in attempting to remove the dead fetus through the normal birth canal, the shoulders had to be broken.

At trial, the physician admitted that had a Caesarean section been performed at noon, there was nothing to suggest that the mother would have had anything other than a normal, live baby, although he stated that it was his practice to let patients progress in labor, even in cases of cephalopelvic disproportion, in order to check their progress. The medical experts, who testified at the trial, concluded that the delay in performing the Caesarean section earlier was a deviation from accepted and applicable standards of practice for obstetricians. And judgment was entered against the physician (38)

B. Negligent Treatment

A doctor is under the general obligation to exercise reasonable skill and judgment in the treatment and care of his patient. What is "reasonable" is usually based on the standard of care which other doctors would exercise under the circumstances.

Throughout this Chapter, we have discussed rather specific forms of medical malpractice. It is important to keep in mind that medical malpractice may involve any conduct that falls below the requisite standard of care that injures the patient. (39) Physical malpractice can thus arise from virtually any *negligent treatment*. What constitutes 'negligent' treatment depends on what the standard of care is. First, remember that mere proof of a bad result, or a mishap, is no evidence of lack of skill or negligence. (40) Further, to establish malpractice, the doctor's negligence, rather than merely the natural process of the underlying disease or injury, must cause the injury for which the patient is suing. (41) What is required, simply, is that the patient demonstrate that the doctor failed to do what the average, reasonable doctor in good standing, practicing in the same or a similar community or hospital, would have done in a similar case. (42)

EXAMPLE: Julie Carman entered into labor with her first child and was sent to the hospital by her doctor. After her arrival, her doctor artificially ruptured Julie's uterine membranes to help speed delivery through an amniotomy. This was the first time her doctor realized that the baby was in a breech position (aftercoming head) as opposed to the normal cephalic position (head first). A previous check of the fetal heart tones had suggested that the baby was in a cephalic position.

Shortly after Julia's membranes were ruptured, a nurse discussed with the doctor the guidelines posted in the labor department by the chief of the department. The guidelines stated that:

Please observe the following suggestions to upgrade the OB Department's performance.
1. No amniotomy unless in labor
2. No amniotomy until presenting part is engaged.
3. All breech –
   a. Pelvimetry should be ordered.
   b. Amniotomy should not be done.

CONSULTATION
Members without full privileges should seek a consultation with a member of the staff with full privileges in the following cases: (primi means first)

1. Primi inductions
2. Primi breech

The doctor and nurse specifically discussed the need for the pelvimetry and the possibility of consultation. The doctor replied that he would base his treatment on the patient's progress and any further findings made during labor. No pelvimetry was taken or consultation made. Although he had full privileges to deliver breech presentation babies, the doctor's privileges were limited such that he did not have the right to perform a Caesarean section and noted that "consultation in complicated and unusual cases will be requested."

21

The doctor did not believe a Caesarean section was necessary although there was some indication, from the baby's heartbeat, of fetal distress. Instead, after delivery started, the doctor performed the accepted 'Mauriceau maneuver' in order to deliver the baby. (43) The legs and trunk of the baby emerged in a timely manner, but the aftercoming head delivery was very difficult and delayed for some ten minutes. No effort was made to pass oxygen to the baby with a catheter even though the delivering doctor was able to put his fingers in the baby's mouth. The doctor subsequently stated that he assumed the cervix clamped down upon the baby's neck after the passage of the trunk.

Medical experts who testified at the trial, testified that piper forceps should have been used, either immediately or when the Mauriceau procedure failed. (44) Piper forceps were not on the instrument tray in the delivery room. The doctor further stated that he had never used Piper forceps before because he had always been able to deliver babies by following the Mauriceau procedure, but did believe he was competent to use them.

After the baby was delivered, breathing did not start spontaneously and resuscitation for a period of 12 to 15 minutes ensued. Another doctor was called for consultation with regard to the baby. The infant died approximately four hours later, apparently from shock and acidosis due to anoxia irreversible cellular exchanges. In its decision, the Court, which had reviewed the case, stated that the doctor was not negligent in failing to seek consultation, but was negligent in his failure to use Piper forceps. (45)

4. GUARANTEED RESULTS AND WARRANTIES

This is another major Cause of Action for medical malpractice suits. This cause of action basically hold that where a physician guarantees or warrants a particular result, he may be liable if that result if not achieved, particularly if elective and non-compulsory treatment is involved.

As elaborately explained in earlier passages in this book, most lawsuits brought against doctors are based largely on negligence. In essence, this means that a doctor generally agrees only to treat his patient with the requisite skill and care. The doctor does not guarantee or warrant any particular result. Nevertheless, a doctor and patient may agree that a particular result will be achieved.

Where this is the case, and a doctor guarantees or warrants a particular result, he is entering into an agreement or contract with a patient. A guarantee or warranty is simply a promise that matters will turn out as the doctor says. It can be oral. It may not require special consideration or payment. (46) If the patient goes ahead with the procedure because of that promise, in such a case he can sue the doctor involved for breach of the guarantee or warranty if the agreed result is not achieved, even if the doctor is not negligent in treating the patient.

Traditionally, the courts have been hesitant to find 'guarantees' or 'warranties' as a cause of action in medical malpractice suits. They recognized that because medicine is an inexact science, a "cure" or a special result is often unattainable regardless of skill. Also, in making statements to a patient, a doctor is often simply "therapeutically reassuring" his patient by refraining from advising him of the manifold dangers attendant to any surgical operation, avoiding a detrimental psychic reaction to the patient that might obstruct successful treatment. (47)

This state of affairs is changing, however. In some states, a number of well-intentioned statements have been held by the courts to be guarantees of one sort or another. *A few examples of such cases, include the following:*

A statement that a proposed resection of an ulcer patient's stomach would take "...care of all your troubles....you can eat as you want to, you can drink as you want to... You can throw your pill away, your Maalox you can throw away..." (48)

A statement that an operation would make a hand 100 percent perfect. (49)

A statement that a cure would be affected by removal of a growth under a certain procedure. (50)

A statement that a prescribed radium treatment on swollen glands in the patient's neck would not leave a permanent scar. (52)

A statement that a plastic surgical procedure would make a patient a model of harmonious perfection, and would be performed without pain or scarring. (53)

A statement that an operation would result in only minor, hairline scarring. (54)

A statement that plastic surgery on a patient's nose would enhance the patient's beauty and improve her appearance. (55) Dentists are particularly subject to these sorts of claims.

EXAMPLE: Josephine Cirafici was examined by her dentist for a complaint of ill-fitting dentures. After the examination, she claimed that the dentist induced her to permit him to install dental implants. According to Josephine, the dentist told her the implants would eliminate the difficulties she was having with her dentures, and that she would be able to eat "corn on the cob" and other foods for which natural teeth are particularly suitable. She agreed to the implants, the patient said, but after some two years the dentist extracted them, however, acknowledging that they were a failure, and replaced them with dentures. During the entire period in which Josephine kept the implants, they were loose and painful and prevented her from eating solid foods.

Under the circumstances, the court found that Josephine could sue the dentist for a breach of a contract or warranty. Of special importance in making the decision was that an elective and non-compulsory treatment was involved and that Josephine was seeking only a refund of the cost of the original procedure and the cost of the new dentures, rather than seeking damages that are ordinarily associated with tort claims (e.g., pain and suffering). (56)

5. PREGNANCY

A principal basis for legal cause of action in malpractice law is pregnancy. A physician has the duty to advise his or her patients of the risks of a prospective child's abnormality, and of the availability of tests to detect abnormality so that an informed decision as to whether to have an abortion can be made.

Wrongful pregnancy and birth or life cases represent a developing area of the medical law. These cases usually result from a failed sterilization, or a failure to genetically diagnose or detect a defect in the fetus. The parents increasingly charge today that if they had been adequately warned, or that if the fetus had been tested, they would have had their unborn child aborted! And because their doctor failed to warn them, the parents would contend, they would have their doctor pay for the extraordinary costs associated with the rearing of the 'defective' child!

Some critics of such cases have made the Solomonic suggestion that parents who bring these claims, especially if the child is normal and healthy, should be asked to bring the unwanted child to the courtroom and, at the opportune time, be handed a hammer and invited to kill the object of their rejection! While such a solution may sound radical, such charges and claims made by parents against the doctors are just as equally offensive to the doctors, more especially to those of them who, though strongly opposed to abortions on moral and religious grounds, are nevertheless being asked by such parents to either acquiesce in such procedure or to encourage or "inform" parents on taking the step.

Different Types of Cases In This Category

It is useful to you, whether you're a parent (the patient) or doctor, to distinguish among the various types of cases which are being brought within this category:

A.   Wrongful pregnancy: In a wrongful pregnancy action, the alleged injury to the parents is the birth of an unplanned or unwanted, but usually normal and healthy, child resulting from the negligence of a doctor or other health care provider in performing an abortion or a sterilization, or in filling a prescription for contraceptives. (57) Wrongful pregnancy cases are sometimes referred to as claims for wrongful conception.

B.   Wrongful Birth: In a wrongful birth action, the injury usually claimed by the parents is the birth of a seriously handicapped or diseased child whose birth might have been prevented were it not for the negligence of those charged with the prenatal testing, genetic prognosticating, and the counseling of the parents as to the likelihood of giving birth to an abnormal or physically or mentally impaired. (58)

C.   Wrongful Life: A wrongful life action, unlike either a wrongful pregnancy or wrongful birth action, is not brought by the parents on their own behalf, but is an action brought by them on behalf of their child. In such an action, it is claimed that because of the doctor's negligence the child's adult life will be burdened with an impaired existence occasioned by the abnormal or unusual health condition with which he must live. (59)

Keeping the concepts of these actions separate and distinct is important because under the law of medical malpractice the liability of the doctor is deemed to vary depending on the type of case brought and the state in which the case is brought.

In a wrongful pregnancy case, a patient or the patient's spouse usually may recover for the expenses incurred for the unsuccessful operation, as well as for the associated 'pain and suffering' involved, for any medical complications caused by the pregnancy, the costs of delivery, lost wages, and loss of consortium (spousal companionship and conjugal relations). (60) On the other hand, where the child is normal and healthy, the parents typically may not recover from the future expenses of raising the child. (61) One court, for example, appropriately recognizes as follows, that:

> In a proper hierarchy of values the benefit of life should not be outweighed by the expense of supporting it. Respect for life and the rights proceeding from it is at the heart of our legal system and, broader still, our civilization. (62)

Or, as recognized by another court: "The existence of a normal, healthy life is an esteemed right under our laws, rather than a compensable wrong." (63)

EXAMPLE: Donna and Leon Cockrum and Edna and Afzal Raja each had children who were healthy and normal. The Cockrums alleged that a vasectomy was negligently performed on Leon. The Rajas alleged that a bilateral tubal cauterization was negligently performed on Edna. Edna apparently suffered from hypertensive cardiac disease and had been informed that it would be medically dangerous for her to have a child. Donna and Edna became pregnant. When Edna showed signs of pregnancy, she was examined at a gynecology clinic, but was advised she was not pregnant. It was not until after it was medically safe to have an abortion that she learned that she was in fact pregnant. Although the Cockrums and Rajas could seek to recover for the pain of childbirth, the time lost in having the child, and the medical expenses involved, they could not recover as damages the future expenses of raising the children. (64)

In a wrongful birth case, as contrasted to a wrongful pregnancy case, parents are not seeking the expenses of raising the child. The child was wanted. However, because they claim that the child would have been aborted had they known of the child's possible defects, they seek to recover from the doctor the extraordinary medical expenses of the child during his minority years. Many states allow recovery of the expenses in these kinds of cases involving the wrongful birth claims. (65)

EXAMPLE: Michael and Nancy Goldberg were expecting a child. Being Jewish, their physician apparently knew that the offspring of Jewish parents had a higher rate than other children to be born with Tay-Sachs disease. (66) The Goldbergs alleged that they were not informed of the possibility of Tay-Sachs disease or of any testing procedures available to determine whether their child would have the disease. No tests were performed. When their son, Jeffrey, was born, it turned out that he had Tay-Sachs disease. If the physician in fact did not inform them of the risk of Tay-Sachs disease, the physician could be held liable for damages, including medical and other expenses reasonably necessary for the care and treatment of the impairment. (67)

A wrongful life case effectively carries the claim for extraordinary expenses in a wrongful birth case to when the child becomes an adult. Some states also allow recovery of these expenses in wrongful life cases. (68) Recovery of the child's pain and suffering due to the defects usually is not allowed. (69)

EXAMPLE: Janice and Thomas Siemieniec brought a suit on behalf of their son, Adam, for extraordinary medical expenses he was expected to incur during his majority years. Adam was a hemophiliac. Prior to his birth, Adam's parents had specifically consulted with their physicians about the risk that Adam would be born a hemophiliac. Janice was concerned about the possibility because two of her cousins were afflicted with the disease. Diagnostic tests were performed in time for Janice to decide whether to abort the pregnancy. One of the physicians subsequently sent a letter, a copy of which was provided to Janice, stating that the risk of Janice being a hemophilia carrier was "very low." Because a physician is under a duty to give a woman accurate professional advice in making an abortion decision, Adams's parents could sue to recover extraordinary medical expenses that he would incur on account of his hemophiliac condition in his adult life. (70)

6. PRESCRIPTIONS

This is yet another major area for a cause of action in medical malpractice. Prescriptions are usually instructions, preferably in writing, by a licensed physician and surgeon to a licensed pharmacist or other qualified person, to dispense or administer drugs to a patient. They may also take the form of instructions to other healthcare providers, such as physical therapists and dietitians. A patient's doctor can be held liable for errors he makes in making such prescriptions.

A physician has an obligation to prescribe or administer to the patient the appropriate medication in proper dosages. Further, a physician has an obligation to warn his patients if the patients' mental or physical abilities will be affected by the medications the patient would consume, either alone or in combination with alcoholic beverages or other items. Within the category of prescriptions malpractice, one of the easier forms of wrongdoing to establish involves prescription or medication errors. This is simply because of the fact that the standard of care required in this area is often easily established, and a deviation from that standard is clear-cut.

An example of medical malpractice in this area, would involve violation of one of the various laws which govern the dispensing of drugs. Doctors are subject to both the federal and state laws and regulations pertaining to controlled substances. (71) Another example of this form of medical malpractice would be when a drug is administered in a manner contrary to the manufacturer's instructions. This may relate to such things as the manner in which the drug is administered (e.g., whether it should be orally or by injection), or right dosage. Violation of a drug manufacturer's explicit instructions regarding the proper manner of administering a drug, and the specific warnings concerning the hazards that may apply in the event of its improper administration, is considered so obviously a malpractice that the patient's attorney usually doesn't even have to offer an expert testimony to establish that the doctor deviated from the proper standard of care required. A basic case is established in such cases merely by showing the manufacturer's instructions. (72)

Still another example of this form of medical malpractice, is based on misunderstood prescriptions. For example, oral prescriptions for a patient may often be given over the telephone to a pharmacist or a hospital nurse, or even as a fleeting direction to a nurse. While oral prescriptions cannot be entirely avoided, the safest way for a doctor to prescribe medications is by written prescription. Written prescriptions are normally made on a printed pad, or in the record of a hospital patient. It is important for the physician to legibly write prescriptions. There is absolutely no excuse for the atrocious penmanship of many doctors. It is surprising that pharmacists and nurses silently tolerate this problem! Usually no remedial action is taken on this until the offender is zapped with a malpractice suit.

A developing dimension of prescription-based medical malpractice is the extent to which a doctor must warn his patient of the extent to which a medication may impair the patient's mental and physical abilities. Significantly, the courts have extended this obligation out of the need to protect those who may be harmed by the patient's actions while mentally or physically impaired.

EXAMPLE: Daniel McCarthy was being treated by two physicians at a hospital. The physicians ordered that McCarthy be given the prescription drugs Prolixin Decanoate and Thorazine. Hospital personnel injected McCarthy with Prolixin Decanoate and gave him a Thorazine for oral consumption. On the same day, McCarthy was discharged from the hospital. He then consumed an alcoholic beverage and drove his automobile with James Kirk as a passenger. Allegedly, the medications diminished McCarthy's mental and physical abilities, which caused McCarthy to lose control of the automobile. As a result, the automobile hit a tree. Kirk suffered severe and permanent injuries in the occurrence. A court held that the physicians had an obligation to warn of the adverse effects of the drugs and that, additionally, this obligation extended to the public for their protection. Therefore, said the Court, Kirk, who was not even the patient of the physician, could sue for his injuries.

7. ABANDONMENT

A physician does not have an obligation to accept a patient. However, once a physician accepts a patient, he must continue to care for him until: 1) the patient is well; 2) the patient discharges the physician, or, 3) the physician withdraws from the case, but only after the patient is given a reasonable time to find substitute care. (74)

In order for an obligation of caring for a patient to arise, a doctor-patient relationship must be established.

A doctor-patient relationship is not established by a doctor by merely giving you an appointment, listening to your complaints, or even performing some cursory examination on you, such as taking your blood pressure and temperature, or listening to your heart tones. After this initial evaluation, a doctor may decide for various reasons that he does not want to take care of you. Without serious danger of legal liability, he can inform you that he does not choose to care for you.

However, if he proceeds from that and extends your examination, or prescribes medicine for you, or sees you on additional visits, he probably has established a doctor-patient relationship. Then he may not then "abandon" you or decline to care for you until, as mentioned above, you get well or fire him. The doctor may withdraw from your case but only after giving you reasonable time to find another doctor.

A common circumstance, in which a doctor's abandonment is claimed, is following some operation or procedure. (75) The duty to continue treating a patient after surgery is not within a doctor's absolute discretion, but is subject to the general standards of the medical profession. (76)

EXAMPLE: Jan Ann Longman was referred by the family dentist to another dentist specializing in oral surgery to have her wisdom teeth removed. All four teeth were removed, two of which required a surgical procedure followed by suturing of the gum. Jean returned to the dentist to have the sutures removed. On the day following removal of the sutures, Jean developed pain and stiffness and swelling of her right jaw. She telephoned the dentist's office to report her condition and to seek his care and assistance. At this point her jaw was very stiff and she could barely move it at all. The oral surgeon's nurse determined that Jean was not having any pain in the area of the extraction itself and so, with the oral surgeon's approval, told Jan to see a medical doctor.

Jean followed the oral surgeon's advice. The physician she consulted suggested that she see her oral surgeon, but when told that his office refused to treat her, provided her treatment. As a result of the medication she received from the consulted physician, she received some temporary relief, but her difficulties persisted. Jean again called her oral surgeon's office, but was again told to see a medical doctor. Her physician again suggested that she see her oral surgeon, but after hearing her relate his telephonic refusal to assist, treatments were repeated. Jean was eventually hospitalized and diagnosed as having an infection of the jawbone known as osteomyelitis. She was treated primarily with steroids and penicillin and her condition eventually improved. (77)

When Jean sued, the court found that the oral surgeon was legally obligated to have continued to care for Jean until the threat of postoperative complications had passed, and that having failed to provide that care, the oral surgeon was liable to her for damages. (78)

8. DISCLOSURE OF RECORDS OF INFORMATION

A. Invasion of Privacy

A patient has a right to reasonable visual and auditory privacy.

Prior to the year 1890, no English or American court had ever recognized what we now call the right of privacy. In that year, there appeared in the Harvard Law Review a famous article by Samuel D. Warren and Louis D. Brandeis, which proposed that right. (79) There are few areas in which the right of privacy is more demanded than in health care.

What is the nature of the patient's right to privacy? If a doctor publicizes information about his patient, particularly if private facts and the disclosure of them would be highly offensive and objectionable to a reasonable person of ordinary sensibilities, this would be deemed an invasion of privacy.

The Joint Commission on Accreditation of Healthcare Organization's Manual for Hospitals specifically recognizes a patient's right to privacy in the hospital setting. It provides that a patient has a right to "be interviewed and examined in surroundings designed to assure reasonable visual and auditory privacy. This includes the right to have a person of one's sex present during certain parts of a physical examination... and the right not to remain disrobed any longer than is required....." (80)

B. Divulgence of Confidential Information

A doctor may not, with certain exceptions, disclose any information he may have acquired in the course of attending a patient in a professional capacity which is necessary to enable him professionally to serve the patient. (81)

Each state recognizes a physician-patient privilege. Under this privilege, a doctor is prohibited, without the patient's consent, to disclose any information provided to the doctor while being treated if necessary for the treatment. Today, the privilege is often considered designed to assure a patient's privacy. The privilege is actually intended to prevent a doctor from testifying against the patient in court. Similar privileges are similarly provided for the clergy, reporters and others.

Of increasing concern to doctors are the increasing incidences in which exceptions are made to the physician-patient privilege. Although variations exist from state to state, a doctor usually may be allowed and, indeed, may be compelled, to release information about his patient in:

> Trials for homicide when the disclosure relates directly to the fact or immediate circumstances of the homicide;

> Actions, (civil or criminal) against the doctor for malpractice;

> With the expressed consent of the patient, or in case of his death or disability of his personal representative or other person authorized to sue for personal injury or of the beneficiary of an insurance policy on his life, health, or physical condition;

> Actions brought by or against the patient, a beneficiary under a policy of insurance, or the executor or administrator of his estate wherein the patient's physical or mental condition is an issue;

> Where an issue is raised as to the validity of a document as a will of the patient;

> Criminal actions were the charge in either murder or abortion, attempted abortion or abortion;

> Actions, civil or criminal, arising from the filing of a report in compliance with the Abused and Neglected Child Reporting Act: (82) or,

> To any department, agency, institution or facility which has custody of the patient pursuant to a State statute or any court order of commitment. (83)

State laws may provide other circumstances where information may or must be released. (84)

C. Defamation

If a doctor is in any way otherwise entitled to disclose information about a patient, nevertheless, he still has an obligation to refrain from making untrue statements which injure the patient's reputation.

Defamation is made up of the twin torts of '*libel*' and '*slander*.' Libel is defamation by written or printed words or pictures, or in a form other than spoken words or gestures. Slander is defamation by oral utterances. In either case, defamation generally involves making an untrue statement which tends to injure a person's reputation in the popular sense; to diminish the esteem, respect, goodwill or confidence in which a person is held; or to excite adverse, derogatory or unpleasant feelings or opinions against him. (85)

Where a defamatory statement is involved, the courts first consider the type of defamation involved. The most serious type, so called per se defamation, involves the imputation of a crime, of a loathsome disease, of lack of chastity, and those affecting a person in his business, trade, profession, office or calling. This type is considered so serious, that the person doesn't even have to prove damages; liability is essentially automatic. In all other cases, some special damage must be shown to have incurred by the person defamed in order for him to sue.

Under some circumstances, a statement may be made even if defamatory. For example, on the floor of the United States Senate, a Senator can say virtually anything he wants in connection with the business at hand, even if false. A Senator is absolutely privileged in that setting.

In addition to an absolute privilege, the courts recognize a qualified privilege. Where a doctor makes a statement in connection with his practice, it may be protected by a qualified privilege. (86) To be protected, the statement must be made in good faith meant to serve a legitimate purpose, such as obtaining payment from the patient's health insurance carrier, and it must be limited in its scope to that purpose. Good faith also implies that the statement be made at a proper time, in a proper manner, and only to the proper parties. (87) If a qualified privilege applies, a communication is actionable only if that privilege has been abused. In general, this requires proof of 'actual malice,' such as actual knowledge that the statement is false or without reasonable grounds for believing the truth of the statement. (88)

Anyone can be accused of defamation. However, doctors are particularly vulnerable, because they are frequently asked for information about a patient which is often of an extremely personal nature. Statements may necessarily fall into the per se categories of defamation involving disease, chastity and work ability. Thus, even where a statement must be made in connection with a doctor's practice, care must be taken.

EXAMPLE: Ruby Edwards was a 14-year-old unmarried girl. Upon consulting a clinic, Ruby's mother authorized the clinic to send the bill for Ruby's medical services directly to her insurer. When the claim form was signed by Ruby's mother, certain portions were not filled in. When completed, a handwritten notation listed Ruby's diagnosis as "atopic pregnancy," an apparent misspelling of ectopic pregnancy which means "the development of the ovum outside the uterine cavity, as in the Fallopian tubes or ovary." The printed form otherwise noted "R/O (rule out) atopic pregnancy." After a problem with the insurer, completed new forms changed these statements and stated that the visit was "Initial Gyne Visit," and that the final diagnosis was "Gyne Exam." Ruby's mother filed suit on her behalf alleging defamatory diagnosis. The court held that the statements that were made were protected by a qualified privilege and that that privilege had not been abused. Only negligence, and not actual malice, was shown. (89)

9. OTHER FORMS OF MEDICAL MALPRACTICE

A. Failure to Protect

Suicide: Where a doctor considers his patient to be a potential suicide risk, the doctor may be under an obligation to take reasonable steps to prevent the patient from harming himself.

When a person commits suicide, his relatives often look to blame someone. Of course, they don't want to blame themselves! If the person was under a doctor's care, the doctor is a common target. If a reasonably skillful physician would consider a patient a suicide risk, a doctor is under an obligation to take reasonable steps to prevent the patient from harming himself.

Victims: When a doctor determines that his patient presents a serious danger of violence to another, he incurs an obligation to use reasonable care to protect the intended victim.

Psychiatrists often deal with patients who present a danger to others. It has been found that when a doctor or other professional determines, or pursuant to the standards of his profession should determine, that his patient presents a serious danger of violence to another, he incurs an obligation to use reasonable care to protect the intended victim against the danger. The discharge of this duty may require the doctor to take one or more of the various steps, depending upon the nature of the case. Thus, it may call for him to warn the intended victim or others likely to apprise the victim of the danger, to notify the police, or to take whatever other steps are reasonably necessary under the circumstances.

EXAMPLE: Prosenjit Podder was being treated by Dr. Lawrence Moore, a psychologist. During the course of his treatment, Podder confided to him an intention to kill an unnamed girl, readily identifiable as Tatiana Tarasoff, when she returned to California after spending the summer in Brazil. Dr. Moore, in consultation with others, decided that Podder should be committed for observation in a mental hospital. He also requested the assistance of the police department in securing Podder's confinement.

When the police officers took Podder into custody, they were satisfied that Podder was rational and so released him on his promise to stay away from Tatiana. Dr. Moore's supervisor then directed that no further action be taken to confine Podder for evaluation. Podder then persuaded Tatiana's brother to share an apartment with him near Tatiana's residence. Shortly after her return from Brazil, Podder, as he stated he would do, went to the residence and killed Tatiana.

The California Supreme Court held that a therapist has a duty to warn a patient's intended victim, or others likely to apprise the victim of the threatened danger. (90)

B. Misrepresentation and Non-Disclosure

Although a doctor has no obligation to disclose or to remedy the effects of prior acts of malpractice, he may not intentionally misrepresent or fraudulently conceal the malpractice.

Attorneys frequently admonish doctors to "come clean" when they commit malpractice. This cleansing ritual is a sure way of inviting a malpractice suit, or to lose one if filed against a doctor. A doctor actually has no obligation to disclose his malpractice. However, if a doctor intentionally misrepresents or fraudulently conceals his malpractice, he may be liable to a patient.

EXAMPLE: Brent Smith apparently required a kidney transplant. The kidney was rejected by Brent's body. Brent was told that it would be impossible for him to obtain a second kidney transplant because the kidney would again be rejected by his body. Brent failed to undergo a second transplant for more than two years. It was then that Brent learned that the first kidney was rejected allegedly because of malpractice and specifically a failure by his doctor to treat infection. Brent sued his doctors claiming that because of the affirmative, intentional misrepresentation regarding his ability to undergo a kidney transplant, he delayed obtaining a proper cure for his condition. The court held that intentional misrepresentation occurring subsequent to malpractice is a separate and distinct claim against Brent's doctors. (91)

C. Infliction of Emotional Distress

A doctor may be liable for emotional distress caused others due to intentional or negligent acts under limited circumstances. A developing area of the law centers around this question: under what circumstances may a person recover damages for disturbances of MENTAL caused by another. Claims of this sort are categorized generally as those for infliction of "emotional" distress. Infliction of emotional distress may be of either intentional or negligent kind. Many states recognize both forms. (92)

Intentional infliction of emotional distress allows a person to recover for mental disturbances resulting from some intentional and outrageous conduct. Although physical impact or injury is usually involved, this is not always essential. (93) Instead, the conduct complained of must be so outrageous, so atrocious and so utterly intolerable that a person of ordinary sensibilities may not reasonably be expected to endure it. (94) The claim may be made by the person against whom an outrageous conduct is directed, as well as by third parties, typically those who are not only present at the time but are known to be present by the perpetrator. Relatives of crime victims, for example, fit this bill as persons who often have a claim for intentional infliction of emotional distress.

Unlike intentional infliction of emotional distress, which is an act resulting from some intentional act, negligent inflection of emotional distress, on the other hand, results from some negligent act. Most claims of this kind are made by a witness to an accident. Although some States will deny a claim for negligently caused emotional distress brought by a bystander unless it is accompanied by a contemporaneous physical injury to or impact on the person making the claim, some states do not. Instead of the "impact rule," other states have adopted the "zone-of-physical-danger rule." Under this latter rule, the person making the claim must be in a zone of physical danger, and must, because of another's negligence, have a reasonable fear for his own safety. This rule does not require that the bystander actually suffer a physical impact or injury at the time of the negligent act, but it does require that he must have been in such proximity to the accident in which the direct victim was physically injured that there was a high risk to him of physical impact. Of course, the bystander must show that he/she incurred some physical injury or illness as a result of the emotional distress caused by the negligence. (95)

It is likely that claims made against doctors for negligent infliction of emotional distress will increase as the law in this area develops. With the present open-door policy to the delivery and operating rooms of our American hospitals, it is entirely possible that claims based on infliction of emotional distress will be made if and when a family member witnesses some act of medical malpractice.

Although many courts have yet to broaden the horizon of emotional distress claims, other courts have already done so. For example, while some courts have thus far denied emotional distress claims in wrongful birth actions, (96) other courts have allowed them. (97)

EXAMPLE: Lee Gibring consulted his family doctor for depression. Lee's doctor referred him to a psychiatrist. The psychiatrist treated Lee on two occasions and instructed him to return a few days later for further treatment. The day before his appointment, Lee committed suicide through carbon monoxide poisoning. Later that day, Lee's wife, Kathleen, found her husband dead in the garage of their home. Kathleen claimed that her husband committed suicide as the result of medical malpractice by both the family doctor and the psychiatrist, and that she suffered great emotional distress from finding her husband dead in the garage. The court held, under the zone-of-physical-danger rule as applied in Illinois, that Kathleen could not base a claim for negligent infliction of emotional distress upon herself, because finding her husband dead did not put she herself in reasonable fear for her own safety. (98)

D. False Imprisonment and Wrongful Commitment

The general law: a doctor may not restrain or confine a patient without his consent, except as permitted by law. False imprisonment, sometimes called false arrest, involves restraining or confining a person without his consent and contrary to law. Imprisonment in this sense does not require stonewalls, iron bars or the like. (99) Rather, the prohibition against false imprisonment protects a person's freedom of movement.

The reality, however, is that few doctors ever get to the point where they can really be accused of false imprisonment. There are stories from a past era of hospitals holding (imprisoning) patients until their bills were paid. However, the greater risk in modern-day medical operations is one of an entirely different type, namely, premature discharge. (100)

The most likely instance where a doctor could face a possible claim of false imprisonment, is where a patient wishes to refuse further treatment which you (the doctor) believe is indicated. As discussed in connection with patient contact, a patient is generally free to accept or to refuse treatment. Where an adult is involved, it is important to be sure to document a refusal of treatment by the patient. However, a doctor should not involuntarily restrain the individual. Where a minor is involved, however, a doctor may contact and inform a family services agency, as a refusal of treatment by the parents on a child's behalf may constitute child neglect. (101)

E. Sexual Misconduct

A physician has a duty to refrain from conduct, including sexual activities, that are detrimental to a patient's well being.

Where a doctor engages in criminal sexual misconduct, he may be prosecuted under the criminal law. There is disagreement as to whether non-criminal sexual misconduct constitutes malpractice. Nevertheless, even that still may give rise to other claims against the doctor or medical institution. Regardless of the uncertainty in the law, engaging in such improprieties are simply too risky an act and asking for trouble.

EXAMPLE: A certified social worker held himself out to the general public as an expert in the field of psychology and mental therapy, including marriage counseling. While counseling a particular couple, the social worker allegedly became emotionally and romantically involved with the wife, had sexual relations with her, and thereafter continued to counsel the husband. The husband sued, complaining that rather than rehabilitation of the couple's marital relationship, the social worker committed malpractice doing just the opposite. The court concluded that the social worker could be sued for malpractice under the circumstances. (102)

10. LOOKING AHEAD: FORMS OF MEDICAL MALPRACTICE IN THE FUTURE

What doctors can be sued for is not a constant or stagnant matter. What is a perfectly good medicine today may be bad medicine and a malpractice tomorrow. Why?

Simply stated, because whether a doctor may be sued for doing or not doing something, is a matter determined by the courts. Very simply, a doctor will be subject to a suit ONLY IF AND WHEN a judge is convinced that in certain generalized circumstances redress should be available because a patient is injured as a result of the actions or inactions of a doctor!

Of course, this is not entirely arbitrary on the part of the judges. Rather, many factors of law and otherwise are considered in deciding whether redress should be available. *The broad factors considered in making this determination include:*

- The extent to which the doctor could or should have anticipated that his actions or inactions would result in the patient's injury. Courts refer to this factor as the extent to which the injury was "foreseeable."

- The magnitude of the burden of guarding against the injury and the consequences of placing that burden upon the doctor.

- The desirability in terms of public policy of imposing a duty on the doctor to guard against the risk that is involved.

The central question here: What will be the novel forms of medical malpractice in the future? According to Melvin M. Belli – reputed to be the "King of Torts" – there are quite a number of areas that are ripe for litigation. *Some of these include:*

Preferred Provider Organizations: Belli considers the preferred provider system ripe for liability claims. For example, when a provider's contract is terminated and a patient still requires care, the doctor could be considered to have abandoned the patient. Similarly, a provider contract may require referrals to other providers although the doctor's standard of care may dictate otherwise. Belli also points out that a doctor's own insurance may not cover the liability arising from provider contacts. (103)

Diagnosis-Related Groups: Under the DRG and similar cost-containment systems, patients may be ousted after the allotted treatment time is up. According to Belli, a doctor has a duty to provide not only care consistent with community standards, but all the care that's medically necessary. Therefore, if a doctor goes along with terminating treatment for financial reasons when the standard of care would dictate that treatment is needed, the doctor could be liable to the patient. (104)

Do Not Resuscitate Orders: Belli points out that "do not resuscitate" orders are a likely problem area. Standards are limited and doctors are reluctant to document these decisions. Belli believes that documentation is essential to avoid problems in this area, including informed statements from family members. (105)

Continuing Education: Medical science develops rapidly, with alternative treatments becoming available all the time. Belli considers a doctor's failure to be knowledgeable of alternative treatments as a significant source of liabilities. It is thus important for doctors to keep up on developments, and constantly so. (106)

Consultations and Referrals: As medicine becomes more specialized, there is a need to better determine when consultations and referrals are required. Belli states that a doctor's hesitancy to seek consultations or make referral boils down to "economics and age." Very simply, the doctor is trying to hold down the patient's costs and keep the patient, or believes he can handle the case. According to Belli, neither of these motivations or beliefs, however, will be placed above good patient care when a medical malpractice claim is made. (107)

Birth Injuries: Belli sees prenatal care and delivery as a particularly risky danger area in the medico-legal limelight. Physicians are being sued at greater rates and the awards are well into the millions. He expects this trend to continue. (108)

Medical Malpractice 101.

CHAPTER IV

THE PRELIMINARY INVOLVEMENT OF THE ATTORNEY
IN A MEDICAL MALPRACTICE CASE

Attorneys are not inclined to work 'pro bono' (meaning, for charity or for nothing). In fact, they frequently lose interest in any case where they don't smell money. They are not interested in a case if you have a less than perfect result that is obviously not malpractice, or if your doctor has merely been rude to you and you simply want to stick it to him! Therefore, before your attorney will agree to accept your case, he will spend a considerable amount of time investigating your charges. In deed, responsible attorneys testify that they turn down far more "malpractice" clients than they accept.

You should realize that while your attorney is gathering up records and investigating and evaluating your charges, your doctor might very well get wind of your intentions. If you still depend on him for care, don't be surprised if you were to get "dumped."

A. PATIENT'S ATTORNEY CONTACT AND CONTRACT

To be sure, there are no doubt cases, where attorneys go to patients and offer to sue doctors (the so-called 'ambulance chaser' attorneys), and hospital employees that tip off attorneys of good prospects. Most suits for medical malpractice, however, usually start with a disgruntled patient going to an attorney's office inquiring about the possibility of suing or demanding to sue.

B. CAUSES OF PATIENTS' INITIAL CONTACT WITH ATTORNEY

Why patients first initiate contact with an attorney varies. However, the common reasons are:

- The result was considered unsatisfactory. The patient may make this determination himself, but very often it is made by relatives and friends of the patient.

- The patient is being pressed for a bill. In a large portion of cases, a complaint of medical malpractice arises when a doctor is trying to collect his bill. At first, the patient cries 'medical malpractice' in order to get out of paying.

- The patient is told by the doctor, a nurse or some other professional, that medical malpractice has actually occurred. In one case, a treating doctor said to the patient, as follows: that "as far as he was concerned, he may have been at fault and that he had an insurance policy of $100,000 for malpractice." And sure enough, the doctor was sued. (1) Perhaps just as often, a nurse or other personnel, particularly in hospitals, may make some suggestive comments to a patient.

Or, in some cases, it is the malpractice attorney who initiates the idea of pursuing a medical malpractice claim. A patient may, for example, have been involved in an automobile accident. The patient actually contacts the attorney with the intent and wish merely to pursue a claim against the person who caused the accident. But the attorney, in the course of attending to the patient's initial primary interest, then begins to make the contention that while the accident may have initially caused the patient's injuries, those injuries, he thought, were negligently treated by the doctor.

C. WHAT HAPPENS WHEN YOU FIRST CONTACT AN ATTORNEY

When you first contact the medical malpractice attorney, he will usually listen and make notes regarding your complaints against your doctor. If he decides it is at least worth investigating, he may enter into a contract with you. Some attorneys wait to enter into a contract until after they have investigated and agreed to take the case. More often, attorneys enter into a contract with the patient, while retaining the prerogative to decline the case after investigation.

Compensation of the Lawyer: The Lawyers' 'Contingency Fee' Deal

Medical malpractice cases are commonly handled by attorneys on a "contingent-fee" basis. In a book to which Mark Twain was a contributor, (2) the contingent fee arrangement was described as follows, in this rather humorous but instructive narrative:

A New Yorker asked Wm. M. Evarts what he would charge for managing a certain law case.
"Well," said Mr. Evarts, "I will take your case on a contingent fee."
"And what is a contingent fee?'
"My dear sir," said Mr. Evarts, mellifluously, "I will tell you what a contingent fee to a lawyer means. If I don't win your suit, I get nothing. If I do win it, you get nothing. "See?"

Many analysts have consistently argued that attorneys are excessively compensated in contingency fee cases. Whether this is so, or, not so, as the lawyers are often adamant to say, we should merely note this here: that the theory behind allowing the contingency-fee arrangement (as the lawyers are often quick to recount!), is to make courts accessible to those who cannot otherwise afford to retain an attorney, by way of sweetening for the lawyer the financial incentive for him to take such cases. According to this theory, this arrangement also takes into account that the risk of losing such cases is high, and hence, it seems only sensible that the attorney should be appropriately compensated, even enticed, for taking that risk. Since the 1850's, the contingent fee has been a unique luxury enjoyed almost exclusively by American attorneys because England, France and most other countries consider it illegal or unethical. (3)

A contingent fee arrangement has been described as one where the amount of the attorney's compensation is 'contingent,' in whole or in part, upon the successful accomplishment (by settlement or by litigation) of the case being handled. (4) The fee arrangement usually must be in writing, and is established by a formula for a fixed amount. (5) Thus, for example, the attorney would typically receive one-third (33%) or 40 percent of the recovery amount.

Most families have had contact with an attorney, perhaps only to buy a house or settle an estate. As a rule, this is the attorney that most patients, perhaps including you, will usually consult. He will listen to you and decide if you have a case. He may then proceed with the case or refer you to another attorney who is more experienced with this type of case.

D. ATTORNEY REFERRAL OF CASES TO OTHER ATTORNEYS, IS BIG BUSINESS

Many doctors would be surprised to learn that the attorney with whom they chatted at the country club or racket club one week, might be the same fellow who plots or encourages a medical malpractice suit the next week. Attorneys manage the feat of staying friends with local doctors, but yet participating in a lucrative malpractice suit by referring it to another attorney, usually in a more remote city.

Most states prohibit the payment of referral fees by attorneys unless the circumstances are disclosed to the client and the client consents to the division of fees between the attorneys. (6) Just how lucrative these arrangements can be was highlighted in one recent case. John I. Lowrey was sued by four attorneys who claimed that they had been solicited to forward medical malpractice and other personal injury cases.

Under their arrangement, Lowrey would receive 60 percent of all collected and they would receive the balance. A medical malpractice case was referred. Two doctors settled it for $410,000, as a result of which Lowrey received attorney's fees of $129,166. He promptly remitted 40 percent, $51,666, to the attorneys. Following a trial of the remainder of the case, a judgment was entered in the amount of $2,500,000, from which Lowrey received $666,666 in attorney's fees. When he refused to forward the 40 percent due the Joliet attorneys, $266,666, they sued. (7) Referrals can mean big bucks!

E. GETTING THE CASE STARTED

On the first appointment, the attorney will listen to your account of the medical or surgical treatment you claim and make notes of them, and, probably, tape record the visit. No doubt, you will also be asked to sign the transcript of the record or prepare a summary.

The attorney may agree on the spot to "take your case" if he considers it to "have merit." What this means, quite simply, is that he thinks he can prove that the medical treatment that you received was a malpractice, that the case against your doctor, if instituted, will yield some money -- to which he will, of course, usually claim up to 40%, plus his expenses!

At this initial visit, the attorney will also evaluate you, particularly if he has had no previous dealings with you. He will decide if you really have been the victim of medical malpractice and suffered an injury, whether you are sincere and will make a believable witness at the courthouse. The attorney may ask you to sign a contract that obligates you to retain him as your attorney as well as other considerations, particularly the financial arrangements.

Even though the attorney may be capable and experienced in handling medical malpractice cases, he may, particularly if you live in a small town, refer your case to an attorney in a distant city. He may still share in any award. The reason for the referral is often to try to keep the local health care providers from knowing that he is your attorney, or that he is representing you in a court case against the doctor. As a matter of course, the reality is that no one likes to be sued, more especially the doctors and hospitals for whom human loyalty, good name and professional reputation matters a great deal. Hence, understanding this, and intending to avoid reprisal, your attorney may find it necessary to reap the financial rewards involved by being surreptitiously involved in your case, while hoping that your doctor or some others in your immediate community, never get to know of his involvement in the case.

1. Records

Following your selection of an attorney (or the attorney's selection for you), the case is "developed" by the attorney. This usually means that a hospital normally must allow a patient or his attorney, after he/she has been discharged, to examine and make photocopies of the hospital records kept in connection with his treatment. (8) The request must be made in writing and be delivered to the administrator of the hospital. (9)

2. Physician Records

Assuming that you presently have, or have had, another physician treating you, other than the one you're suing, a request to examine the current physician's records often follows your attorney's request for the hospital's records. Most states require that doctors allow a patient or his attorney to examine and copy the patient's records. The request (to your present doctor or hospital) must be made in writing and delivered to the doctor. The doctor is obligated to respond within a reasonable time and is entitled to be reimbursed for all reasonable expenses incurred in connection with the examination or copying. (10)

PLEASE TAKE NOTE OF THIS: If you are the patient, you must understand that whenever medical or hospital records are requested, it is ordinarily assumed by all concerned (the doctor to whom the request is made, the hospital, nurse, patient, his attorney, etc) that the possibility of a malpractice claim is being considered. Hence, if your current doctor (or hospital) gets your request letter for records, it is very likely that he'll immediately think that you are considering a legal action against him. You, or the attorney you engage, may avoid the creation or lingering of this kind of impression, however. You should simply talk to or otherwise inform the doctor in advance and explain, for example, that a personal injury claim is being pursued against another doctor or hospital. Indeed, if such an explanation is not provided your other doctor, the doctor may possibly drop you as a patient. And please, don't ever forget that doctors aren't at all comforted by the fact that you are presumably happy with his own performance today, but plan to make a claim against another physician!

F. EVALUATING THE CASE

Your attorney (the one you've engaged on the case) will follow a definite protocol in evaluating your complaints. He will want to find out if your doctor's care violates the essentials necessary to prevail in a medical malpractice suit, namely:

Duty: Was there a doctor/patient relationship between you and the doctor? Was he responsible for your care?

Negligence: Did your doctor deviate from the appropriate standard of care-usually employed in your community?

Damage: Were you in fact injured by the negligence of your doctor?

Cause: Was your doctor's action or inaction directly responsible for your injury?

NOTE: Remember that in Chapter II, we emphasized that the above-listed factors are the four critical "elements" which you must be prepared to prove in court, and that unless you're reasonably certain that you can prove these four elements, you'll have no case against your doctor, and your medical malpractice suit would fail (if you were to bring one)!

Consequently, your attorney will go down the line, one-by-one, on each of the above-listed "elements" of a medical malpractice suit, and explain and fully explore each of them with you as it relates to your own case.

1. **On DUTY:** It is usually simple to determine that your doctor had a duty to you, if he has treated or is treating you.

2. **On NEGLIGENCE:** Has your doctor breached the relevant standard of care? Your attorney will now try to determine, from what you say and the information in the records, if there is a case. As pointed out immediately in the above passage, we discussed elaborately in Chapter II, what constitutes the legal elements of a medical malpractice case (i.e., duty, negligence, damages and causation). A most important and relevant chapter, certainly, in the context of our current discussions! Nevertheless, we wish to emphasize here, for the purposes of the current chapter, that the single most critical question considered in most cases of medical malpractice, is this: whether your doctor breached the required standard of care.

The operative rule and law on this is simple: once a doctor accepts a patient, he automatically has the obligation and duty to use a reasonable amount of care and skill to treat the patient. This doesn't mean that he is necessarily required to possess the highest order of professional qualification in his field which some may have attained. But only that he possess the standard or degree of skill and care which is ordinarily possessed by the members of his profession. This standard of care is determined under the so-called "locality rule" principle by what a reasonably competent doctor practicing in the same community, or in a similar one, would do under the same set of circumstances. (11)

Securing The Medical Expert Witness, The Critical Factor

Therefore, as a major part of your new attorney's overall, initial evaluation of your case, the attorney will now try to determine for himself, from what you've told him and the information in the records, this critical question: will he be able to find an expert witness who will feel convinced enough about the validity of your case that he'll be willing to say that the required standard of care was breached in your case?

As has been repeatedly stated above in this chapter, as well as in others (see Chapter II, among others), the essential standard of care which doctors are expected to meet, is normally determined by an expert witness. In other words, what this means in simple terms, is that if a doctor is said to be guilty of malpractice, then another doctor must agree. (12) To put it another way, *ultimately, unless you can find some other credible physicians who will say that the medical treatment or procedure employed by the patient's doctor is contrary to the essential standard of care which doctors are expected to meet for the given community, you simply can't make a case for malpractice against the patient's doctor!* In sum, one fundamental thing that your own attorney must be able to do, is to determine whether he can find an expert witness for your case – for the case, the specific facts and information, you've presented to him!

Will your attorney have much difficulty finding such a doctor who will willingly accept to testify in the case as an expert witness? It's interesting to note, that at one time in the past, attorneys complained that it was nearly impossible to get one doctor to testify against another. They referred to this as a "conspiracy of silence." Not so anymore, however! In deed, even the famous Melvin M. Belli, who made a highly lucrative career of suing doctors, acknowledges that the old conspiracy of silence has broken down in modern times, and that today more and more topflight specialists are making themselves available as expert witnesses. (13)

In today's malpractice climate, by and large experts are readily available. The basic reality for most medical malpractice legal practitioners is that most attorneys who handle medical malpractice cases usually have their own favorite medical consultants. Some firms even have a stable of these persons. They not only evaluate the case from a medical-legal standpoint, but frequently function as hired guns as the case develops. These days, attorneys also regularly receive advertisements from experts. The *ABA Journal*, the official magazine of the American Bar Association, actually has a classified advertisement section that is dedicated to "Litigation Support, Medical." Excerpts from one recent issue gives one some idea of just how available experts are:

- Medical malpractice litigation consultant available to advise, assist or associate. Experience: eight years and seven thousand cases. Board-certified in surgery....
- Emergency room medical specialist, consultation/testimony....
- Medical and hospital malpractice, personal injury, product liability. Since 1976 we have assisted 4,000 attorneys with 10,000 cases and have been directly responsible for obtaining plaintiffs' recoveries in excess of $100,000,000. 1,650 board certified independent experts in every specialty, nationwide and all states, to review medical records and testify. We can help finance your medical malpractice...cases. Free literature and books......
- Dental malpractice. Consultation, testimony.....
- Orthopedic surgeons. Medical malpractice evaluation/testimony.....
- Neurosurgeon/neurologist. Consultation/testimony....
- Medical devise cases....
- Experienced M.D., J.D., professor of urology. Co-counsel or expert witness....
- Doctors do commit malpractice! Medi-legal experts prove it everyday...
- Podiatric Malpractice Consultants.....(14)

Furthermore, there are also many well-meaning colleagues, particularly young and inexperienced doctors, who have unrealistic expectations of the therapeutic outcomes and can be trapped by a smooth-talking attorney into making a statement, or writing a letter, that could establish a medical standard of care that few, if any, experienced practitioners could attain. Thus, they fall under being expert witnesses.

3. **On DAMAGE:** That you sustained some injury or damages by reason of your doctor's negligence.

4. **On CAUSE:** That your doctor's action (or inaction) was the cause of your injury.

(A SAMPLE - MEDICAL CONSULTANT'S STATEMENT)
**EXPERT DOCTOR'S/CONSULTANT'S
CERTIFICATION FOR AN ACTION IN MEDICAL MALPRACTICE
PURSUANT TO 735 ILCS 5/2-622**

RE: Patient Agnes Doe, minor, V. Dr. Malpractice Davidson

I am a physician licensed to practice medicine in all of its branches. I am board-certified in Obstetrics, Gynecology and Maternal Fetal Medicine. I have reviewed in detail the records, facts, and other relevant materials pertaining to the above patients. I am knowledgeable on the medical issues involved in this matter. My practice is exclusively limited to obstetrics, gynecology and maternal fetal medicine. I have practiced in these areas of medicine for well over the last six years and was in active practice at the time of this review. I am familiar with the appropriate standard of care for a reasonably well-qualified obstetrician/gynecologist, as well as the standard of care for an obstetrical nurse.

For the reasons set forth below, it is my opinion, which I hold to a reasonable degree of medical certainty, that there is a reasonable and meritorious basis for suit against Dr. Malpractice Davidson:

1. Inappropriately applied a vacuum extractor before the plaintiff, ... was at the recommended +2 station.

2. Failed to utilize all of the appropriate delivery maneuvers recommended for a shoulder dystocia patient.

3. Failed to utilize all of the appropriate delivery maneuvers again after they failed the first time.

It is my opinion that the above listed acts and omissions constitute a failure to comply with the appropriate standard of care for a reasonably well-qualified physician; it is further my opinion, to a reasonable degree of medical certainty, that the aforementioned deviation from the standard of care by Dr. Malpractice Davidson, caused injuries to Patient Agnes Doe, on (date)...

SIGNED: Dr. John Consultant

IN THE CIRCUIT COURT OF THE EIGHTH JUDICIAL CIRCUIT, ADAMS COUNTY, ILLINOIS

Plaintiffs,

No.

Defendants.

Attorney's PLAINTIFF'S 735 ILCS 5/2-622 AFFIDAVIT

I, John J. Attorney Esq., first being duly sworn, state as follows:

1. I am the attorney for the Plaintiffs.

2. I have consulted with a medical doctor who I reasonably believe is familiar with the relevant issues involved in this particular action, has practiced in the same area of health care and medicine that is at issue in this action for more than 6 years and who I reasonably believe is qualified by his experience to render opinions in the subject area of this case.

3. The reviewing health care provider has determined in a written report, after review of the medical records of the within named Plaintiffs and other relevant materials involved in this action, that there is a reasonable and meritorious cause for the filing of such action against XYZ Hospital and Malpractice Davidson, the Defendant in this action.

4. I reasonably believe that the reviewing doctor is knowledgeable as to the appropriate standards of care in cases like this involving the Plaintiff minor.

SIGNED: John J. Attorney Esq., attorney for plaintiffs

How The Lawyers Hire & Work With The Medical Expert On Your Case

Actually, after your attorney's preliminary interview of you and their evaluation of your story and your medical records, their next major order of business, would be their work with the medical experts. Before your lawyer would ever file a lawsuit against the doctor, he would usually have hired an expert or experts who are knowledgeable in the medical specialty of your doctor, or another practitioner in the field, to read the record, analyze your situation, and give them an 'expert' opinion as to the merits of your case (i.e., whether the required standard of care was breached by the doctor). These persons, often called "consultants" at this stage of the case, are then frequently used as 'expert witnesses' against the doctor at the trial stage.

If you are the patient involved in a malpractice case, and you wonder whether there's anything at all you can possibly do to help the expert witness in your case become even more effective, the answer is that there is. Apparently, attorneys seldom suggest it, but it has been highly recommended by lawyers who specialize in medical malpractice litigations, that patients should themselves meet with and evaluate, independently, the expert that is selected. Why? Because, it is said, after all, the expert's testimony will eventually be evaluated by other laymen, the jury. Hence, your own personal view may be just as reliable!

What If, Possibly, You Can't Get An Expert For Your Case?

If you can't get an expert, is this possibly a case where an expert isn't needed? To be sure, an attorney usually wants and, indeed, needs an expert in order to establish the doctor's required standard of care and his breach of that standard. There have been cases and instances, though, where patients' attorneys, unable to find a suitable expert to render needed testimony in the case, moan and groan and try to squeeze around the expert testimony requirement by rehashing the "conspiracy of silence" theory. Under some circumstances, courts have listened and will accept something less.

G. SOME ALTERNATIVES WHEN NO EXPERTS ARE AVAILABLE

The Legal Doctrine of Res Ipsa Loguitur

Where, in very rare cases, expert testimony is possibly not available, or an expert is hesitant to testify, the attorney will search for an alternative method to establish medical malpractice.

One method to establish medical malpractice without expert testimony, or with something less than eager testimony, is to use circumstantial evidence. The most common type of circumstantial evidence is that which is given the name of res ipsa loquitur. This Latin phrase, which simply means, "the thing speaks for itself," is the offspring of a casual work of Baron Pollock during argument with another attorney in a 1963 case in which a barrel of flour rolled out of a warehouse window and fell upon a passing pedestrian. (15) In its inception, the principle was nothing more than a reasonable conclusion, from the circumstances of an unusual accident, that the person sued was probably negligent. (16) And the argument or reasoning which immediately flows from this, therefore, is simply this: that from those given circumstances in the case, a judge or jury could infer or assume that someone was negligent.

To take advantage of this inference, what must be shown? (17)

- You, the plaintiff, must show that you were injured in an occurrence which would not have occurred in the absence of negligence. This element may be shown by means of expert testimony, or, in an appropriate situation, may be within the common knowledge of laymen. For example, a doctor reluctant to testify against another is often more willing to say that a particular injury would not ordinarily occur if proper care is exercised, than to say that a fellow doctor was negligent. Proof of an unusual or unexpected medical result which ordinarily does not occur in the absence of negligence, will also suffice to allow the application of the res ipsa loquitur doctrine. (18)

- You must show that you were injured by an instrumentality or agency under the management or control of the person sued. For example, when a patient submits himself to the care of a hospital and its staff, and is rendered unconscious for the purpose of undergoing surgery that's performed by independent contracting surgeons, the patient has demonstrated the necessary control. (19)

- The patient must show that he was injured under circumstances which were not due to any voluntary act on the part of the patient, or of any negligence on his or her own part.

A dramatic but real example of where the res ipsa loquitur doctrine is applicable is where sponges or instruments are left in the abdomen from surgery. (20)

H. USE OF SOME OTHER METHODS IN NO-EXPERT WITNESS SITUATIONS

If an expert witness is not available and the res ipsa loquitur doctrine does not apply, patient's attorneys will then attempt to find a written procedure, explicit instructions from a drug manufacturer, or some other resource, to help establish the standard of care. (21) Examples of these resources include the following:

- Physician Desk Reference (PDR)
- Federal Drug Administration (FDA) releases
- Equipment manufacturers' instructions
- Hospital or clinic bylaws, rules or regulations
- Standards or guidelines adopted by organizations to which a doctor might be a member
- Books and journals in the field

Of these resources, the Physician's Desk Reference is particularly significant because it is available to every attorney and layman. (The FDA releases and equipment manufacturers' instructions have basically the same objective as the Physician's Desk Reference) It is important that we identify exactly what this publication is. It is simply a compilation of the package inserts prepared by the manufacturers' drug attorneys listing every possible reaction to the drug, meant for the purpose not only of complying with the FDA regulations, but also of protecting the drug company from legal attacks for any adverse reactions. The responsibility, then, is laid on the prescribing doctor with: "The advantage must be weighed against....etc," or something to that effect. Virtually every doctor has had the experience of a detail man coming into his office and orally telling a story about a product, that is entirely different from what appears on the insert. Furthermore, if the medical doctor were to follow every precaution, and do every test that such inserts mandates, it would be at the prohibitively high cost and expense in time and money to the patient. Nevertheless, doctors are all too well aware of the "bottom line reality" involved in such matters: namely, if these instructions are not followed, and something goes wrong, the doctor is in peril.

Uses of hospital or clinic bylaws, rules or regulations in court trials

Every organization likes to establish standards or rules of one sort or another. They give the organization status and suggest that all of its staff or members are 24 karat gold. This is a most dangerous trap for the gullible doctor.

A prime example is the bylaws, rules and regulations, of a hospital medical-dental staff. There is a temptation to nitpick and codify a Utopian set of rules which defy strict compliance. However, attorneys are quick to take advantage of this.

In the landmark Illinois case, Darling vs. Charleston Community Memorial Hospital, (22) the Illinois Supreme Court ruled that a hospital's standard of care was to be determined not only by reference to the standard of practice of other hospitals in the community, but also by reference to the hospital's own bylaws and other written standards of practice.

If you are a doctor involved in a malpractice case, or potentially so in your professional practice, chances are that you are probably a member of some professional organizations or boards. It is highly advisable that you read any so-called 'standards' promulgated for or by that organization or board, very carefully and be prepared to testify at your trial that these are merely ideals, and that its total attainment is illusive, was never intended to be fully attained, and even impossible. You should make a strong, and, even preferably, emotional case that you, as a medical professional and practitioner, would love for everyone to be in perpetual good health and to live forever. And, furthermore, that the reason most medical care continues to improve is because we are continuing to strive for goals that seem impossible at a given moment in time.

As the patient's doctor on trial, you should come fully aware that it is not unusual for your patient's attorney to ask you, at the trial of the case in court, whether you are familiar with this or that author on medical or malpractice issues, and then smoothly proceed to hold up a well-known book or journal and ask if you are familiar with the publication. By that, the attorney is probably trying to get you to admit that book, journal or written article, is an authoritative item that is well recognized and widely accepted by the medical profession! But here comes the hidden trap: the attorney may then read a passage that would establish a 'standard of care,' and then attempt to prove that you, as a doctor, breached that standard!

For the doctor, here's a simple rule always to bear in mind. When faced with a malpractice suit, it is vital that you constantly keep in mind the extent and content of the material that your patient's attorney is digesting and preparing to use against you, and that you yourself anticipate, timely get a hold of, and know this same material backward, forward and upside down, so as to avoid being trapped.

I. HAS THE STATUTE OF LIMITATIONS RUN OUT IN THE CASE?

Every State has statutes which limit the time within which a lawsuit must be filed. These are known as the 'statutes of limitations.' An attorney evaluating a case will determine whether the statute of limitations has elapsed, or ran as attorneys call it.

The applicable statutes applicable vary from state to state. Increasingly, special limitations for malpractice cases have been adopted. They usually range from two to five years. For minors, the limitation may well not begin to run until obtaining adulthood.

J. WHAT REALLY DETERMINES WHETHER THE ATTORNEY TAKES YOUR CASE OR NOT?

All right. Let's just assume this is the big question the lawyer you had contacted to take your case against your doctor ultimately comes to: 'Do I really want to take this case?' A relevant question because, in the end an attorney concludes his review of your case by deciding whether he wants to take the case or not.

Actually, the brutal but realistic fact of this matter, is quite simple. Simply put, the decision on this usually boils down to one thing: whether there is any MONEY in the case. Attorneys look for two basic categories of money – lots and easy. If there's lots of money or damages at stake, an attorney would usually take the case, even if the accused doctor's liability is not absolutely clear. On the other hand, if there is not "lots' of money involved, an attorney may be unwilling to take the case (if he has anything else to do), unless there is "easy" money involved. Such a case may be one that has clear liability, but limited damages. A major reason this is almost certain to be the case, is because of one significant internal dynamic that has become the very part-and-parcel of the malpractice and personal injury industry today. What is it? Simply the reality, now widely observed and acknowledged by malpractice attorneys, the doctors' and hospital insurers, and others, that by and large the insurance companies today would eagerly settle virtually any claim, however lacking in any merit it is, for what is called a case's 'nuisance value'! Simply put, the insurance companies, figuring that it will cost them a few, perhaps several, thousands of dollars to litigate and defend even a bogus case, would often quickly "settle" them with the patient's lawyer who comes knocking, even if they know quite well that the patient's claim has virtually no merits at all! Consequently, virtually all a lawyer will need to do, and he would have been assured of collecting something on a particular medical malpractice claim, even of the most bogus kind, is to threaten 'lawsuit,' 'lawsuit' against the doctor! On this, the insurance companies, it seems, have done a great disservice to the doctors today! For, as has been noted by some analysts on the subject, "the best reputation an insurance company or a doctor can have with attorneys, is 'when you sue me, you'll earn every cent you get.' This won't prevent the truly meritorious cases from being filed. But it will prevent nuisance cases."

Finally, it should be noted that, fortunately, there seems to be a brighter light emerging on the horizon on this subject matter. Observers have noted that in more recent years, the decision of the attorney as to whether to take a case, has begun to show some elements of the attorney's own evaluation of the client, himself, as to the merits, or lack of merits of the case. Just as doctors are urged to be most careful in who they pick for their patients, so also are attorneys now increasingly being warned to be very careful in picking their clients. There just may be some underlying risks and hazards in play here even for the attorney himself! Take, for example, a client who has a borderline case at best, and still wants to sue his doctor. Guess what? He might well want to sue his attorney next - YOU!

K. SETTLEMENT EFFORTS & PROCEDURES FOLLOWED BY THE ATTORNEY BEFORE HE/SHE ACTUALLY FILES SUIT

Once an attorney decides to take a medical malpractice case, he does not usually rush to court and file suit as his opening volley against the doctor – unless, of course, the statute of limitations is about to run out. Instead, he will usually write to the doctor and explain that his client plans to sue, and request the doctor to have his insurance carrier contact him for an effort and possibility to settle the case. To make such a letter (or letters) especially effective and intimidating, an attorney may include the draft of the written complaint he plans to file. It has been shown that, as a rule, when the doctor first sees a Legal Complaint, cast in its usual, stilted, often ominous looking and threatening language of the law, it does make quite an impression upon the doctor. (23)

The obvious purpose of these letters is, as such letters would often expressly state, to initiate settlement negotiations with the doctor's insurance carrier – if the doctor has any insurance. As explained in the preceding Section I above, for many, many cases, the primary, underlying intent of the patient's attorney, any way, is probably to get some quick settlement on the case from the doctor's insurers, rather than necessarily to litigate and to drag the matter into court for too long. Further, these letters also serve the subtle role of smoking out ironclad defenses and, possibly, some admissions from the doctor.

Finally, another developing but important factor these days, which bears some weight to the lawyers in how they initiate or conduct their cases in malpractice claims, is a common belief within the legal profession that the courts are starting to deal more harshly with the 'frivolous' kinds of cases – cases which clearly are obviously baseless and have little, if any, merit, but seem to be brought by the lawyer, anyway, essentially to harass, blackmail, intimidate, and exhaust the doctor (the doctor's insurance carrier) into submission, or else. At one time in the past, the courts were manifestly full of "good 'ole boys'" of lawyers and judges who were from the same law schools, and so forth. Today, however, by and large the judges are now much more professional and considerably less tolerant of attorneys who abuse the system. Lawyers would now be expected to know, for example, that if an attorney allows a doctor the opportunity to correct any misunderstanding before a suit is filed, and even if the doctor doesn't, it's less likely under such circumstances, that the doctor can thereafter claim that the case was frivolous.

STATE OF ILLINOIS   )
) SS
COUNTY OF ADAMS   )

IN THE CIRCUIT COURT OF THE EIGHTH JUDICIAL CIRCUIT,
ADAMS COUN TY, ILLINOIS

Glen & Hultz
Clerk Circuit Court 8th Judicial Circuit
ILLINOIS, ADAMS CO.

Plaintiffs,	)))))))))))))
v.	No. t
Defendants.	

ATTORNEY'S AFFIDAVIT IN SUPPORT OF FILING CASE

I, _____ , being first duly sworn under oath, state as follows:

1.   That I am the attorney primarily responsible for the prosecution of the above-entitled case.

2.   That on behalf the Plaintiff we hereby request money damages in excess of $50,000.00, the minimum jurisdictional level of the Law Division of the Circuit Court of Adams County, Illinois.

FURTHER, AFFIANT SAYETH NAUGHT.

_____

SUBSCRIBED AND SWORN TO
before me I

_____
    Notary Public

"OFFICIAL SEAL"

NOTARY PUBLIC STATE OF ILLINOIS

CHAPTER V

CERTAIN PRELIMINARY PROCEDURES THAT MAY TAKE PLACE BEFORE AN ACTUAL LAWSUIT HAPPENS

A. CERTAIN PRE-SUIT PROCEDURES REQUIRED IN SOME STATES

If a case is not settled, some preliminaries to filing suit may exist. Some states have them, while others do not. The nature of pre-suit procedures vary. They are increasingly common, however. The purpose of these procedures is to reduce the number of frivolous or unwarranted cases against doctors. Under most pre-suit procedures, a claim is submitted to a panel, which decides whether the claim has sufficient merit to allow a suit to be filed. Some states have the panel suggest a settlement.

Pre-suit procedures have cut down on the number of malpractice cases. They do so by requiring a patient to pay a doctor's attorney fees if the patient is subsequently unsuccessful in the suit.

B. FILING THE LAW SUIT: HERE ARE THE PROCEDURES

a.   Generally

If settlement efforts have been exhaustively made, but failed, and the patient desires to pursue the case, then the attorney will next file a suit. This is the last step before the battle begins.

b.   The American Legal and Judicial System

In order for a society to function smoothly, it must not only establish rules of conduct, but also a mechanism for settling disputes. The sources of the rules of conduct are the United States and state constitutions, federal and state statutes (enacted laws), and rules and regulations by administrative agencies, and, finally, decisions of the courts. All these rules are called, 'laws.' The people or voters adopt constitutions. The United States Congress and the state legislature adopt statutes and authorize its various agencies to adopt regulations. And, in the process of interpreting and applying these laws, judges render the decisions of the courts.

In the United States, there are actually two separate court systems – the Federal and the State. Medical malpractice cases against doctors are usually filed in the STATE courts.

Whether a court will, or, for that matter, can, hear a particular case depends on whether the court has the legal authority to hear the case. This is called the 'jurisdiction' of a court. The jurisdiction of Federal and State courts differs in some respect. The primary purpose and, therefore, the jurisdiction, of the Federal courts, is to interpret and apply Federal law. If a doctor violates federal narcotics laws, the Federal courts would be the court that hears that dispute, because federal law is involved. If a case has nothing to do with Federal law, however, the Federal courts would not get involved. Medical malpractice cases rarely involve Federal law, however, and so are not filed in the Federal courts.

C. THE FEDERAL JUDICIAL JURISDICTION

There is one instance where The Federal courts have jurisdiction primarily to hear cases which do not involve Federal law. When the United States was founded, the individual States were very independent. Citizens from one State, who were sued in another State, thought they would be railroaded. And so, the United States Constitution allowed the Federal courts to hear cases involving citizens of different States, even if and where Federal law was not involved. (24) This is called the "diversity jurisdiction" principle, meaning that it requires diversity of residence by citizens in different states. In effect, this means that where a doctor who resides in one State treats a patient from another State, it's possible for him to be sued in a Federal court. However, this still remains unusual, unless a national manufacturer of drugs or equipments is also involved.

D. THE STATE JUDICIAL SYSTEM

Most medical malpractice cases are brought in the State courts. The state court system is composed of three tiers. The initial level of this system is, usually, the "District" or "Circuit" court. The District or Circuit court is the trial court of 'general jurisdiction.' This means that most cases begin there. Thus, if you sued for medical malpractice, you will sue in the local District or Circuit court.

Above the local court, in the judicial ladder, is the 'Appellate' court. The purpose of the Appellate court, is to correct any mistakes made at the circuit court level that are brought to the Appellate Court's attention. As such, the appellate court never hears testimony, but merely reviews written records from the case for the purpose of flushing out any technical issues of law and mistakes. The Appellate Court Justices hear the appeal and decide the points raised by a majority rule. In most states there is an absolute right to appeal a case to the appellate court.

At the top of the judicial ladder, is the State Supreme Court. The Supreme Court is the highest court of a state. In some states (the major one among them is New York), other names are used to designate the State's highest court. The Supreme Court of the state considers only those cases that it desires to review, consequently, for that reason the appellate court is effectively the highest appeal available for most cases. (Similarly, the United States Supreme Court hears only those cases, involving Federal issues, which it desires to review.)

E. WHERE THE SUIT IS FILED: THE VENUE

Attorneys, of course, would generally love to be able to sue in any locality they might want. However, they simply may not do so. Rather, although the same courts in different localities within the State may have the same "jurisdiction" (the same power) as any other to hear a case, a suit must be filed in a particular local court. The term "venue" refers to the proper local court where the suit is permitted to be filed.

What is the proper venue in your case where your case should, and is likely to be, filed? Generally, the VENUE in a case is the county of residence of the party sued, or, alternatively, the county in which the issue involved took place. If all the defendants in the case are nonresidents of the State, then the suit may be commenced in any county within your (the Plaintiff's) State. Where a corporation is the party sued, such as a drug manufacturer, it may be sued wherever it has an office, or doing business. What this means, is that where a doctor, a hospital, and all others involved in a case, are from the same State's county, they must be sued in that county. If they are from several counties, they may be sued in any of the counties where one of them resides.

As a practical matter, malpractice lawyers will often confide to confidants that there are some counties which are more disposed to granting big awards in cases, than others. Consequently, attorneys have been known to do some jurisdiction shopping around – 'forum shopping,' it is called – to pick the 'best' court possible to sue in, within the contest, of course, of the proper venue for the case.

To be able to expand the attorney's selection of the counties wherein a suit could be filed, one ploy the attorney may employ, may be to look to sue people in as many counties as possible. For example, say a patient is transferred to a regional health center, or sent to another doctor in a different county simply for consultation, the attorney may try to tie the new hospital or doctor to the case, thereby creating yet another county in which a suit can be brought. Similarly, if a drug manufacturer can be brought in as a defendant in the case, then the number of counties from which to choose are expanded considerably.

The Original Venue Could Be Adjusted In Order To Get The Proper One

After the suit is filed, your attorney will determine whether the venue used is proper. Where it is determined not to be proper, or that the parties have been sued as a sham just to establish venue in a particular county, the attorney may ask to have the case transferred to another county, such as where you, the patient or the doctor, live. Furthermore, in many States and court jurisdictions across America today, the courts are now trying to do something about the 'forum shopping' acts by lawyers, and it's not uncommon today to find cases where the courts transfer cases that are filed in one county's court to another court, ruling that that is a more convenient or appropriate place in which to consider the case. For example, say the only reason given why a case is filed in a particular county, is because it is claimed that a drug manufacturer has its office there, though all the other persons sued in the case are in another jurisdictional locale, such as where the patient was treated. Then, the court may simply transfer the case to that other locale where the rest of the defendants are, even though, in technical terms, the original venue is still a proper venue.

F. PREPARING AND FILING THE COMPAINT

While determining where to sue, your attorney will prepare a formal legal document known as a COMPLAINT against the doctor and others to be sued. As the name suggests, a complaint sets forth your "*complaints*" or claims against the parties being sued. In some states, this same document, is called a 'PETITION.' The complaint is then filed with the court in the State and county having the right jurisdiction and venue in which the case is to be heard. And, thereafter, the Complaint (together with the Summons paper and other documents) are formally 'served' upon (i.e., delivered to) the defendant parties sued, in order to commence the legal suit. (See Chapter VI, at Section A, thereof, for more on the summons and the complaint).

G. PURSUING THE CASE

By the time when the suit is filed, your attorney will usually have:
- Heard, and apparently accepted, your story.
- Reviewed the hospital and medical records.
- Had the records reviewed by another doctor or comparable consultant.
- Determined that the statute of limitations has not run out on the case.
- Decided that there is merit (or money) in the case.
- Determined what is the proper jurisdiction and venue for the case.

From these basics above, your attorney will continue to develop the case. Your attorney has investigated, studied your case and decided that you really have a case that is worth pursuing. He will then explain to you the steps that will be required in order to expect to prevail with a favorable verdict in the end.

NOTE: Before directing your attorney to proceed with the case, be sure to pay close attention to the explanation he offers you as to what a lawsuit will involve, and decide if the effort is all worth it, or that you can really take it! Be aware that this matter is going to involve a great deal of effort on your part, that includes your appearance and testimony in court. Also, know very well that doctors and hospitals do not take lawsuits kindly; furthermore, though this, as with most attorneys, will probably be of little or no importance to your attorneys, fully realize that, particularly if your residence is in a small town, this action will end your relationship with your doctor, and he will have no interest whatsoever in caring for you and your family in the future.

Hospitals, as well, have the same attitude. Other health care providers will also know about your suit, and they may be reluctant to care for you. This is understandable because this country is grid locked in a medical malpractice crisis, which is fueled by patients who generally regard the health care delivery system as being under the control of greedy moneygrubbers, and that the only recourse that a patient has is the medical malpractice suit.

What This Suit Could Mean To The Life & Future of the Doctor

A medical malpractice suit, even if the defendant (the doctor) prevails, permanently changes the attitude of the doctor for the rest of his life. Any altruistic inclinations he might have had all his/her life before that, disappear, and that doctor now considers every patient a potential malpractice litigant.

If you are a patient who has sued, or is contemplating suing, your doctor, you may be told by malpractice attorneys that doctors carry malpractice insurance, and, therefore, that it will really not cost the doctor anything. That's simply hogwash! There's absolutely no truth or an ounce of reality to that. Quite the contrary is actually the case. What is actually true, is that, in the first place, some doctors do not even carry malpractice insurance at all, the cost is just too high (frequently some one-third of their gross incomes), that they simply cannot afford carrying one. Indeed, for some doctors, that may even mean stopping the practice of medicine altogether, or, at least, the performance of certain high-risk specialties, such as obstetrics and neurosurgery. What could be more distressing than to see oneself, train, prepare, and sharpen your skills into some of the most highly schooled and trained professionals of his society, only for him or her to involuntarily give it all up after a wrenching malpractice suit, including facing a shattered reputation and career and financial doom!

The patients, themselves, though this is hardly apparent or immediate to them, wind up ultimately paying for this in one way or another when it's all said and done.

After you have considered all of these things, you must make this decision: 'Do I really want to proceed with a malpractice suit'? If you decide to continue, then read on.

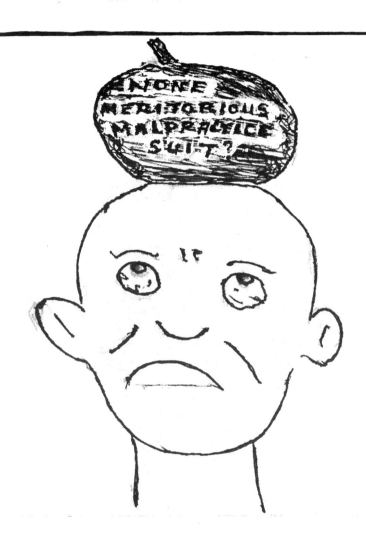

KNOCK IT OFF.

SEE HOW FAR YOU WILL GET.

THEN

GET YOURSELF ANOTHER DOCTOR.

IF

YOU CAN FIND ONE.

Attorney cross-examination of witness!

President George W. Bush, signing the Class Action Fairness
Act (CAFA), the biggest tort reform of its kind in American history,
in Feb. 2005. (Photo from Mike France's Special Report, "How To Fix The
Tort Reform System," courtesy, *Business Week*, March 14, 2005)

CHAPTER VI

THE LAWSUIT IS FILED: THE BATTLE BEGINS

Procedures In Filing the Lawsuit

Assuming you direct your attorney to proceed with the lawsuit, the following are the steps he customarily follows:

A. THE PRELIMINARY DOCUMENTS FOR THE LAW SUIT

The attorney will prepare a Summons, the legal document, which states that you are accusing your doctor of medical malpractice. He is ordered to appear in court and answer your charges, and instructed that if you win, he should expect paying you a great deal of money.

1. The Summons

The Summons is a document, a formal notice from the Clerk of the Court, advising your doctor that you have filed a suit accusing him of committing some acts of medical malpractice. (See a sample copy of the Summons reproduced on pp 66) The plaintiff's (patient's) attorney prepares and "files" (registers) this document at the court clerk's office located in the town and county where he plans to bring your doctor (the 'defendant') to trial. In the legalistic language of the Summons (and the Complaint), the doctor's patient (or whoever is bringing the suit), is designated as the "plaintiff." And the doctor (or whoever is being sued), and each party against whom the suit is brought, is designated as a "defendant."

The "Summons" is a threatening document. Attached to it, is the COMPLAINT that lists all of the "charges," all the horrible things you are charging that your doctor did to you. You are, in a word, legally notifying your doctor that, according to you (and/or your attorney), you think he committed malpractice. In the end, you will demand that he pay you a huge amount of money.

The Court Clerk acknowledges the receipt of the Summons from your attorney, instructs the Sheriff or a Deputy, typically in full uniform, with a .357 magnum and handcuffs strapped to his midriff, or another process server, to go "serve" the Summons upon the doctor and/or hospital. The sheriff struts into your doctor's office, frequently in full view of his staff and patients, he surprises the unsuspecting doctor with the documents, and "serves" him with the Summons. You can imagine the shock and traumatic impact this has on this totally unsuspecting doctor!

2. The Complaint

Attached to the Summons, is another document called the "Complaint." (See sample copy of a Complaint reproduced on pp.68) The complaint charges one or more of the forms of medical malpractice discussed earlier. If more than one form of malpractice is claimed, the complaint will separate them and set forth each form in separate "counts."

At the end of the complaint (or each count), there is stated just what you want done. This is known as the "prayer for relief." A claim for money damages in the prayer for relief, is referred to as the *ad danum*. Most significantly, the Complaint states that it is MONEY that you, the doctor's patient, want as a "remedy" for the "awful" things that your doctor did to you. And not, for example, remedies like having the State officials take away the doctor's license to practice, which would really get to the heart of the doctor's professional "incompetence," since that would prevent him from being able to injure the attorney's present client or anyone else ever again!

The point is that attorneys, particularly those practicing in the medical (and other) malpractice industry field, are hardly hesitant or shy in making it rather crystal clear, that they are in this whole malpractice business merely for the buck. Their interest in your case, many of them will even openly tell you, is basically MONEY – one-third to 40-50 percent of what you get from your doctor, plus expenses. Indeed, they'll often declare to clients, to defending doctors, and to their critics and others alike, that they have no interest in dispensing "welfare" or "public interest" (not getting paid) cases. True to that line of thinking, for years, it was customary in most states, for example, for malpractice lawyers to list on the Complaint a catalog of outrageous demands for millions and millions of dollars, even though the attorney had no expectation of getting anything even remotely approaching such amounts. The purpose? Simply a strategy ploy on the part of the lawyers to condition the jurors' and the judges' minds into granting their clients outrageous malpractice awards. When prospective jurors, for example, read such inflated demands and figures, the lawyers calculated, that would have them exited and thinking that the patient had in fact been extraordinarily abused, that his doctor was a pure quack, and that the patient, therefore, was entitled to far more money than in 'normal' or 'ordinary' cases! In recent times, however, over decades of objections by defendants (doctors') attorneys, patients' attorneys are now forbidden from listing exaggerated claims on patients' Complaints, and may only list a nominal amount designed merely to classify the claim for court purposes, such as a figure like 'more than $15,000.'

B. THE IMMEDIATE PERSONAL REACTIONS OF A SUED DOCTOR

The growing reality of today is that for most doctors in practice in America, the day is likely to come in their lifetimes, when they will be actually sued for medical malpractice. One thing they can be absolutely certain of about it, though, is this: it is a day that they are not likely ever to forget!

Anticipating that a medical malpractice suit will be filed against you, or even that one is about to be filed against you, is a wrenching enough feeling that is so depressing and frightening already. But, even more so, to a doctor, there is no feeling which could compare with actually being sued, actually being served with a summons for malpractice. It is of critical importance that the patient should realize the equally critical significance of this!

1. The Emotional, Psychological, Financial, & Other Impacts of Suit On a Doctor
What happens with a doctor, a man or woman probably well respected and revered in his community, who has just received a summons for malpractice? Immediately after receiving and reading the summons, most doctors are numb and in shock. Matters get even worse for the doctor because such a service of the Summons is often preceded, or

followed, by a public notice in the local newspaper publicly announcing this. To be sure, to hear the malpractice lawyers, the immediate impression might be that a doctor who is suddenly greeted with a summons, would almost certainly take a stoic, nonchalant, "I'm not worried, the insurance company will take care of it" attitude, and forget all about it! In reality, though, that's far, far from the actual fact. Quite to the contrary, experts report that such doctors react as though they've been hit with an unexpected, sudden, fatal disease. Such doctors, used to being viewed as solid citizens and 'stand up' professionals and the pillars in their community, may, at first, try putting up a tough outside appearance, and going through the motions of continuing to maintain their practice. But they are barely able to function. Sleepless nights and days of nightmare follow. They are gripped with an almost crippling fear of being ruined professionally in terms of their professional reputation, of being totally wiped out financially. He immediately becomes bitter, defensive, and begins to regard every patient with suspicion as a potential adversary and litigant. Indeed, so traumatized and scarred do such doctors become from this experience, that even if exonerated in the end, there will still remain some permanent emotional and psychosomatic scars left with them probably for the rest of their lives. (1)

The emotional states that a doctor goes through after being sued for medical malpractice, has been aptly described as a variation of the grief reaction, as follows:

- Shock and disbelief
- Fear of impending doom
- Anger, particularly toward the legal system, the practitioners and the doctor's former patients
- Attempt to carry on
- Desire to retaliate (e.g. sue for malicious prosecution)

Finally, on this point, how is this for "justice" and "fairness" for doctors, eh? That even if in the end the sued doctor endures all the trauma and virtual torture of a trial and is able to survive, and is ultimately vindicated and proven absolutely clean with no wrongdoing whatsoever to the patient, still the permanent scar to his psyche, the devastation to his reputation and professional integrity, much less his practice, is rarely compensated, not even worthy of a single letter of apology from the patient or his attorney!

2. The Immediate Legal Reaction and Defense Posture of The Sued Doctor

Typically, the doctor will move quite quickly to consult with and engage his own attorney to defend him. Doctors are told by their attorneys (defense or defendant's attorneys) to try to let the above-listed first three stages slide by quickly and move into a "resolve to fight" mode. Patient's (plaintiff's) attorneys, particularly if the claim is a frivolous one, are, in fact, counting precisely on using the lawyer's massive 'shock effect' ploy to panic your doctor into a quick settlement. These days, however, fortunately for the doctors, unlike the situation which existed not too long ago, nowadays most doctors would hardly succumb to this ploy. The health care delivery system is at the end of its string and the doctors and other professionals involved in it seem increasingly convinced that the only way the present medical malpractice carnage can be stopped, is for the doctors and the hospitals themselves to adopt a 'never surrender' attitude. There is a growing resolve within the health care delivery system that every frivolous malpractice suit brought against a doctor must be vigorously pursued to a total victory, or otherwise be prepared to face destruction at the hands of the lawyers and the law!

C. WHO IS THE PLAINTIFF OR THE SUING PARTY IN THE CASE?

Most often, the person who sues a doctor will be his own patient. This is not always the case, however. If a minor (a person under 18 years of age for most states) is involved and no legal guardian has been appointed for him, a parent or other adult person can sue for the minor as his "next friend." A next friend is simply a person who brings a suit on behalf of a minor without having been formally appointed his legal guardian. If a minor has had a legal guardian appointed to manage his estate, then his legal guardian would be the party to bring the suit on his behalf. (4) [For other sections of relevance, see Chapter III, Section 1(f), "Consent for or By Minors," as well as Section 1(g) thereof].

Previously, if the patient dies as a result of medical malpractice or before a claim is resolved, the right to sue is traditionally terminated. Thus, purely in technical legal terms, it could be reasoned that it would be better to negligently kill someone than main him! This has since changed, however, with the adoption of the wrongful death statute. Under this law, the legal representative (e.g., the executor or administrator) of a decedent's estate, may file a suit on behalf of the decedent's next-of-kin, or the decedent's next-of-kin can sue on their own. Such a suit seeks to recover the pecuniary losses resulting from the death, such as lost support.

Under most circumstances, those indirectly injured as a result of medical malpractice, may bring their own action against a doctor. Thus, for example, if a wife is unable, or unwilling, to engage in sexual relations with her husband because of some medical malpractice, the husband may be able to sue for 'loss of consortium,' meaning the conjugal fellowship of husband and wife.

Although rarely done, doctors may be named in medical malpractice cases as "respondents in discovery" in some states. This procedure permits a patient's attorney to name a respondent in discovery if he believes the person has information essential to determining who should be sued. The purpose of this provision is to stop attorneys from suing everyone in sight. If named as a respondent in a discovery, the doctor must disclose information as if sued, and it is likely he might be joined as a defendant. Thus, such legal maneuver is often a close cousin to getting actually sued.

D. DUTY OF DOCTOR TO NOTIFY HIS INSURANCE CARRIER UPON SUIT

After being served with a summons (or any other claims), your doctor or his attorney, will usually notify his insurance carrier (if any) and provide a copy of the summons and the attachments. All policies include this requirement. If the doctor fails to give such a notice, the carrier may be able to deny coverage.

E. THE DOCTOR REVIEWS THE SUIT & CHARGES AGAINST HIM

After the doctor has calmed down – at least as much as he can, until the case is resolved – he settles down to study what bad things he has been accused of having done to his patient. First, he will thoroughly review the Complaint and the charges that the patient (the patient's attorney) made in the Complaint. He will obtain copies of, and assemble, all records related to the case. He will then prepare a detailed statement for his insurance carrier (assuming, of course, that he has insurance), and for the attorney retained to represent him.

Just what will be in the statement that he prepares? It will all depend on the nature of what the patient is accusing him of. However, the doctor will need to keep in mind the four elements of a medical malpractice case that the patient will be required to prove in order to prevail in a malpractice case. (see, basically, Chapter II, and Chapter IV, Section F).

- Did the doctor incur a duty to care for the named patient (i.e., was there a doctor-patient relationship)?
- Was the doctor negligent, that is, did he (she) deviate from the appropriate standard of care?
- Was the patient injured? – Damages
- Was the doctor's negligence, if in fact there was any, the "proximate" (i.e., direct) cause of those injuries or damages claimed?

Keeping these elements in mind, the doctor will organize his answers to the complaint. Here are the areas the patient should consider, as well.

- **Introduction:** The doctor will keep in mind that this statement is being prepared to assist the insurance carrier, if he has insurance, and its attorney, in defending the Complaint that the patient filed against him. He will focus on providing any relevant background in the filing that can be used against the patient in defending himself.

  He will determine if he really had a doctor-patient relationship with this patient.

  He will inquire if there is any gossip, notoriety, or other information that his insurance company should know about concerning the patient and his family (e.g., psychological, financial, etc.) He will check if he has a credit report on the patient's family. He will investigate if the patient or his family has been involved in any other suits.

  He will review his record to determine when he first started treating this patient for anything. He will review what he treated the patient for in the past.

  When did he first start treating the patient for the matter raised in the complaint?

  When is the last time he saw the patient? Is he currently treating the patient for anything? How will he end any relationship with the patient?

- **Negligence:** The doctor will try to respond to your (the patient's) charge of negligence. He will try to anticipate what your attorney will say to build a case against him. Your doctor will consider these questions:

  What exactly is the negligence or form of medical malpractice claimed?

What did the doctor treat you for?

What is the standard of care for the treatment that he should have followed in treating the patient for the ailment involved?

How did the doctor decide what the standard of care is? If it is based on any written documents (e.g., drug manufacturer instructions, hospital bylaws, books, etc.), he should locate copies of those.

Did he follow the standard of care?

If he followed the standard of care, how did he do so?

If he did not follow the standard of care in all respects, how did he not do so?

Did his treatment vary from the standard of care generally used in the area?

Does you doctor consider himself negligent in this case?

- **Experts:** Because of the fact that proof of negligence usually requires expert testimony, the doctor will want to know what experts you, the patient, are relying on. The patient's doctor will consider these questions:

Did another doctor treat you at the same time he did? If so, who?

Did another doctor or a nurse treat you after he did? If so, who are they?

Did another doctor or a nurse make any comments regarding your doctor's treatment?

Is there anything in the records which raise some question as to the doctor's treatment? If so, highlight that record.

Is there any other likely expert of whom you are aware?

Does any of these doctors or individuals have any personal dispute or grudge with patient's doctor?

- **Damages:** The doctor will explain his views on the "injury" or "damages." He will consider these questions:

Did he injure or harm you, the patient?

Is he aware of any additional treatment which you had to undergo because of what he did or didn't do?

- **Causation:** Did he, the patient's doctor, actually cause the injury or damages which you complain of? He will consider these questions:

64

Would your condition be the same regardless of whether he was negligent?

Was your injury caused by someone else, including another doctor?

Did you take his advice or treatment, or did you refuse treatment?

- **Records:** The doctor will collect copies of all his own records and those to which he has access (e.g., hospital records) regarding the case, regardless of whether he considers them important or not.

- **Complaint:** the doctor will again review the Complaint and, provide any comments he might have, paragraph by paragraph, on each and every statement made. He is careful not to admit any error in what is alleged in the complaint, however slight.

- **Attorney:** The doctor will record what he knows about the attorney who represents you, the patient. He will consider these questions:

Does he know that attorney?

What is the attorney's reputation?

Is the attorney known to take frivolous cases, or does he sue only if he knows he can win?

Has he had any dispute in the past with the attorney?

- **Summary:** The sued doctor will conclude by offering to meet with the carrier's agent or the attorney it has selected to defend him at any time to discuss the case.

PATIENT, PLEASE NOTE: You may rest assured of this: that the minute your doctor receives the Summons indicating that you (the patient) are suing him, this suit will be his constant concern, a 24-hour-a-day affair with him, and if he considers it frivolous, that will even intensify his anger and determination to win will crescendo!

STATE OF ILLINOIS   )
) SS
COUNTY OF ADAMS   )

FILED

Clerk Circuit Court 8th Judicial Circuit
ILLINOIS, ADAMS CO.

IN THE CIRCUIT COURT OF THE EIGHTH JUDICIAL CIRCUIT,
ADAMS COUNTY, ILLINOIS

)
)
)
        Plaintiffs,   )
)
v.   )   No.
)
)
)
)
        Defendants.   )

PLAINTIFF'S
DEMAND FOR JURY TRIAL

_____
Attorney for Plaintiffs

THE STATE OF NEW JERSEY , TO THE ABOVE NAMED DEPENDANT:

SUMMONS WITH NOTICE

YOU ARE HEREBY SUMMONED in a Civil Action in the Superior Court of New Jersey, instituted by the above named Plaintiffs, and you are whereupon required to serve upon the said Plaintiffs, whose name and address appear above, either (1) an Acknowledgment of Service hereof, or (2) an Appearance, or (3) an Answer to the annexed Complaint, within 20/35* days after the service of the Summons and COMPLAINT upon you, exclusive of the day of service. If you fail to do so, Judgment by Default may berendered against you for the relief demanded in the Complaint. You shall promptly file your Acknowledgment of Service, Appearance, or Answer, and proof of service thereof, in duplicate, with the Superior Court, at this address:

. . . .

in accordance with the rules of Civil Procedure.

DATED: ....200.....

Clerk of the Superior Court

Defendant's
Weight: _____
Age:
Color of Hair:
Color of Eyes:
Distinguishing Marks:
Residence:
Place of Employment:

IN THE CIRCUIT COURT OF THE EIGHTH CIRCUIT JUDICIAL ADAMS

Patient Agnes Doe, minor
Plaintiffs,

CIRCUIT,

v.

XYZ Hospital
Malpractice Davidson,
Defendants

COMPLAINT AT LAW

Complaint

COUNT ONE

COUNTY,

ILLINOIS

LINOIS, ADAMS CO.

NOW COMES the Plaintiffs, Patient Mary Doe, and Patient Agnes Doe, Minor, through their attorneys, John J. Attorney Esq., and complaining of the Defendants, Dr. Malpractice Davidson, states as follows:

1. That on   (date), and at all times material, Defendant, Malpractice Davidson, was a physician licensed to practice medicine in all its branches by the State of Illinois.

2. That on   (date), and at all times material, Defendant Malpractice Davidson was member of the medical staff at the XYZ Hospital in Quincy, Illinois.

3. That on   (date), Defendant, Dr. Malpractice Davidson, was an agent and/or employee of the XYZ Hospital

4. That on   (date), the Plaintiff, Patient Mary Doe, was admitted to the said XYZ Hospital as an obstetrics patient.

5. That Plaintiff, Patient Agnes Doe, a minor, was delivered on (date)

6. That Patient Agnes D, a minor, was under the care of Defendant Malpractice Davidson, and by and through its agents including XYZ Hospital during the pregnancy, labor and delivery

7. That at all times material herein, Defendant Malpractice Davidson held himself out to the Plaintiff and the public generally to be a specialist in Obstetrics and Gynecology.

8. That in treating the Plaintiff, Patient Agnes Doe, a minor, the Defendants, XYZ Hospital and Malpractice Davidson, by and through its agents and/or employees, had a duty to possess and apply the knowledge and use the skill and care which reasonably well-qualified

9. That the Defendants, XYZ Hospital and Malpractice Davidson, by and through the acts of its agent and/or employees, including Malpractice Davidson, while treating Patient Mary Doe, and Patient Agnes Doe, a minor, were negligent in one or more of the following respects:

    a. Failed to adequately perform a vaginal delivery;
    b. Failed to perform a cesarean section;
    c. Failed to adequately treat the minor's shoulder dystocia;
    d. Failed to adequately monitor labor;
    e. Negligently performed a vaginal delivery by exerting excessive downward traction;
    f. Negligently applied a vacuum extractor before the Plaintiff, was at the recommended plus 2 station
    g. Negligently failed to perform delivery maneuvers before initiating excessive downward traction.

10. That as a proximate result of one or more of the foregoing negligent acts or omissions of Defendants, Patient Agnes Doe, the minor Plaintiff, was severely injured; she has been injured both internally and externally; she is permanently disfigured and disabled; she has and will experience pain and suffering; she has and will incur medical expenses; and she has an impaired earning capacity or will be incapable of earning a living.

11. The Plaintiffs attach an affidavit and report in compliance with 735 ILCS 5/2-622 (See Exhibit "A").

WHEREFORE, the Plaintiff, Patient Agnes Doe, a minor, by Patient Mary Doe, her parent and next friend, demands judgment against the Defendants, XYZ Hospital and Malpractice Davidson, in that sum of money in excess of the minimum jurisdictional level for the law division of the Circuit Court of Adams County.

COUNT TWO
(Family Expense Act)

NOW COME the Plaintiffs, Patient Agnes Doe, a minor, by Patient Mary Doe, her Parent-and-Next Friend, and Patient Mary Doe, individually and collectively, and complaining of the Defendants, state:

1-10.   The Plaintiffs, Patient Agnes Doe, a minor, by Patient Mary Doe, and Patient Mary Doe, restate and incorporate, by reference, paragraphs 1 through 10 of Count One of this Complaint at Law as paragraphs 1 through 10 of Count Two of this Complaint at Law, including all subparagraphs, as though fully set forth 11.   That the Plaintiff, Patient Agnes Doe, is a minor, and Plaintiffs, Patient Mary Doe and John Doe, are her lawful parents and legal guardians, and as such, have been liable for substantial medical and care taking expenses arising out of Patient Agnes Doe's injuries.

WHEREFORE, Plaintiffs, Patient Agnes Doe's, a minor, by and through her parent and next friend, Patient Mary Doe and John Doe, Individually, demand judgment against the Defendants, XYZ Hospital and Malpractice Davidson in an amount of money in excess of the minimum jurisdictional level of the law division of the Circuit Court of Adams County, Illinois.

SIGNED: John J. Attorney Esq.,

Attorney for Plaintiffs

PRE-

A. THE FRAMING OF HIS DE...

First, on the part of the patient, afte...
have caused the Summons to be served o...
him that this is not just a dream but that yo...
minimum, make it a point to make sure that ...
case and concluded that you have a good reaso...
medical malpractice, and that he truly genuinely
courthouse..

On the doctor's part, after the doctor has been hit w...   ...Complaint
and it's now crystal clear to him or her that he has been ...   ...g malpractice
acts against his patient, the next step for the patient, of cou...   ...n to wait and see
what the doctor comes up with as his response and defense ...   ...atient's charges. As the
patient, at that stage you (the patient) and your attorney are usually locked in a temporary
stalemate, anticipating, even anxiously, the response of your doctor.

The Two Basic Grounds for Defense of a Case: the 'Law' and the 'Facts'

All court cases are defended on two basic grounds: either on the 'legal grounds,' or on
'the facts' of the case. At the initial stages of a case, the "legal" grounds are the most likely
ways for a defending party in a case to get a claim rejected in the court process. And then,
at the trial stage, the "facts" become the critical aspect.

Defenses Based On The Legal Grounds

The legal grounds, on which a patient's suit can be rejected, are numerous. The doctor's
attorney, being skilled in the law, would be expected to recognize this, and to pursue these
"legal technicalities" on the doctor's behalf. The common legal grounds raised, include
these:
- **Statute of Limitations Expires:** The case has to have been filed before the Statute
  of Limitations expires. If the statute has run out, the case will be dismissed
  routinely by the court. (1)
- **Prerequisite Not Followed:** The patient, or his attorney, must follow any state law
  prerequisites that are relevant to the suit; and in the event that these have not been
  complied with, the case is to be dismissed. (2)
- **Good Samaritan Statutes Applicable:** To encourage doctors to provide
  gratuitous medical care in cases of emergency and under certain other limited
  circumstances, most states have adopted several so-called Good Samaritan statutes.
  These statutes include those which prohibit doctors from being sued on account of
  gratuitous emergency care provided the injured persons. (3)

71

PRE-TRIAL SKIRMISHES

Defenses based on the Facts

- Patient's Actions:
  injury: A patient wh...
  cause his...
  ent...

ient may be responsible, at least in part, for his own
o ignores his doctor's advice, who fails to keep appointments,
ow directions given, etc., can greatly contribute to, or, indeed,
ner injury. The patient's negligence will usually not defeat a claim
ely, but can reduce the amount of his damages. Most states apply what is
known as the theory of 'comparative negligence' liability. (4) That is, damages are
apportioned between the parties involved on the basis of how much fault is to be
assigned to each party. For example, if the injured party contributed to his injuries
to the extent of, say, 20 percent, then the damages are reduced to that amount. In
sum, it's an important question to determine this: 'Is there any blame which could
be placed on the patient'?

- **Assumption of Risk:** It is sometimes suggested that since a patient shall have
  been told, through, for example, an informed consent method, of all the horrible
  things that could happen to him, then he should not be able to sue if one of those
  things do in fact happen. The theory says that the patient assumed the risk of injury
  by undergoing the treatment. This defense usually may not be raised in medical
  malpractice cases. (5) However, there are certain risks inherent to every treatment.
  In defending your lawsuit, a doctor would consider whether what you complain of
  is simply an anticipated result of the treatment, or is something which, but for
  negligence, would not have occurred. In other words, is the injury complained of a
  natural and expected result of the treatment?

- **Standard of Care:** Remember that for your doctor to be found negligent, he must
  have violated the standard of care used in a similar community. (6) The doctor is in
  a much better position than your attorney is, to know what this (the standard of
  care) is, and why. What is the standard of care, and did the doctor conform with it?

B. RESPONDING TO THE COMPLAINT

1. Motions directed to the Complaint

After the sued doctor has been served with a summons, the doctor's attorney will advise
the court, usually in written form, that he represents the doctor. This is done by the
doctor's attorney filing an "entry of appearance" form with the court, or some other written
response to the complaint.

In most tort cases, an attorney will initially respond by filing with the court a written
response (called a "motion"), challenging your right to bring the suit against the doctor, or
the procedure used in doing so. A motion is simply a request addressed to the court to do
something. The type or contents of the motion filed, will depend in large part on the case
involved. However, the most common purpose for such a motion is to ask the court to
dismiss the case for one reason or another. The court might be asked, for example, to
dismiss the case because the statute of limitations had expired. Very often, the doctor's
attorney will argue that the facts alleged in the complaint are not sufficient to state a claim
or cause of action against the doctor. For example, say a claim is being made in a wrongful
pregnancy case for the future expenses of raising a normal and healthy child in Illinois.

Then that case will almost certainly be dismissed if the Illinois state laws do not allow suits for these sort of expenses.

If such a motion is made, and the court grants it, then it will enter an order or decision to that effect. Sometimes, based on such a motion, a case is thrown out immediately and completely. This is rare, however. More often, what is likely to happen is that such a case might be dismissed, but then the patient is given an opportunity to correct his mistakes. He then "amends" his complaint to correct the given errors. When that is done, the motion process starts all over again until finally the complaint is legally sufficient to allege medical malpractice against the doctor.

For a person not accustomed to how the courts operate, these procedures and maneuvers at the initial stages of a case, might seem petty and confusing, more like the rituals of Oriental wrestlers, than an expeditious or serious way to settle a dispute. Properly going through such procedures are important to the sued doctor, however, and often critical to his proper defense of the case. In fact, in some cases, they can result in a prompt termination of the case. Even more important, from the standpoint of the sued doctor, even if they do not end the matter, these motions can pin you (the patient) down on what your complaint is. In the long run, this will make it easier for the doctor and his attorney to defend the case.

2. Answering the Complaint

The patient's Complaint makes allegations of what his/her doctor supposedly did or didn't do. Eventually, the doctor's attorney will file what is known as an "answer" to these allegations. An ANSWER, is simply the document that responds to what is claimed against the accused person. The answer will "admit" or "deny" each allegation made in the complaint. (See pp. **94** for a sample copy of an ANSWER to a Complaint).

When an answer is filed with the court and served on the defendant party, the parties are said to be "at issue." This means that the Complaint and the Answer, when examined together, tell what the parties dispute.

3. Other Pleadings

The answer is often the only pleading filed by a medical malpractice defendant, other than, perhaps, some preliminary actions. Under some circumstances, other pleadings may be needed. The nature of other pleadings can vary considerably.

Some are included as part of the answer itself. Examples include:

- **Affirmative Defenses:** An affirmative defense, is some matter which could result in the patient's claim being denied, even if true. For example, if the case has been settled, and the patient signed a release, the existence of the release document would be an 'affirmative defense.' It is important to note, however, that releases signed prior to, or as a condition of, receiving medical treatment, are usually void.

- **Counterclaims:** If your doctor has some reason to sue you (the patient) back, he may do so as part of the same case. His claim is called a 'counterclaim.'

Although rarely done, if you, the patient, did not pay your doctor's bill, he could counterclaim for what you owe him. A doctor sued for medical malpractice often wants to "counterclaim" against the patient, or his attorney, for bringing the suit against him. This use of the term is inappropriate in this context, however, and such a claim cannot even be considered unless and until after the doctor wins the suit brought against him, if at all.

- **Cross-claims:** Where there are other defendants (more than one defendant) in the case, the doctor may have some claims against them. This is called a 'cross-claim.' For example, a doctor may have followed some drug manufacturer's instructions explicitly, and his patient is injured. If both the doctor and the manufacturer are sued, the doctor may, himself, sue the manufacturer for any damages imposed against him. The term is also used synonymously with counterclaim.

- **Third-Party Complaint:** A third-party complaint is a suit filed against another person who is not a part of the case. Such a complaint serves a similar purpose as a cross-claim, if the person sued is not already named in the case.

- **Jury Demand:** You, the patient, will likely have requested a jury trial. If you have not, and you desire a jury trial, your attorney can demand one. If you have already done so, the doctor need not ask for a jury trial. If you thereafter waive a jury trial, then the doctor will have another opportunity to demand one.

If other pleadings are filed, the patient or other person against whom they are directed, will have an opportunity to 'answer' or reply to them.

C. 'DISCOVERY' OF FACTS & INFORMATION

Generally:

When the pleading stage is completed, or well underway, the parties begin "discovery" process. This is the process that attorneys use to find out ("discover") information relevant to the claims made. The early investigation of a case on both sides is somewhat informal. After the suit has begun, then at this stage formal methods, methods which are enforceable by the court, apply. The methods of discovery to be followed in such a process are prescribed by the courts and include such things like written interrogatories, oral or written questions, discovery or inspection of documents, and physical and mental examination of persons. Failure to comply with the discovery requirements, can subject a party to court-imposed sanctions, ranging from an award of attorney's fees, to preventing a party from maintaining a claim or a defense.

Just what may be 'discovered' in a case, is very broadly construed, just about anything goes. On a patient's side, a patient may obtain from the doctor (and the doctor may also obtain from the patient), any matter relevant for him to any claim or defense. However, when and as necessary, the court may enter an appropriate order – a 'protective order' – regulating discovery to prevent unreasonable annoyance, expense, embarrassment, disadvantage, or oppression.

Although what can be discovered is broad, there are, nevertheless, some exceptions.

74

There is no right, for example, to conduct discovery on privileged communications between a party or his agent and the attorney for the party. Additionally, material prepared in preparation for the trial, is not subject to discovery, if it contains or discloses the party's theories, mental impressions, or litigation plans. Based on these exceptions, the detailed statement prepared for the doctor's insurance carrier and his attorney, cannot be obtained by the patient's attorney.

1. Interrogatories

Interrogatories are written questions regarding the case submitted by one party, such as the patient, to another party, such as the doctor. The person to whom they are directed must answer them in writing, under oath, and provide those answers to all other parties to the case.

If you, the patient, ask your doctor to respond to some interrogatories, he has the advantage of being able to answer them in writing and with some leisure. When the doctor's attorney receives them, he will usually send them to the doctor and suggest to him that he prepare initial answers on the questions. He will then sit down with the doctor, in person, to go over the doctor's answers. The lawyer will then prepare more lawyer-like answers, saying only a minimum, and only in the way which will best support the doctor's position. The doctor's lawyer will then prepare the final, written answers to the interrogatories, he will submit those answers to the doctor for a final review and the doctor's signature.

On the doctor's part, the doctor's attorney will usually decide whether he should submit interrogatories to you, the patient, or other parties. Interrogatories are best used to obtain data and objective information, like the amount of bills incurred, names or particulars of other doctors consulted, and the like.

2. Depositions

Depositions are the most commonly used method of discovery in medical malpractice cases. Unlike interrogatories, which are questions submitted and answered in writing, depositions usually involve questions posed orally, and are answered orally. The relevant general rule is that a deposition may be taken of a arty to the case, as well as any other persons having information relevant to the case, such as expert witnesses. Indeed, the present defendant doctor may have already had an experience, previously, with depositions, in a different case in which he might have served merely as a witness or an information-giver. For example, in somewhat more pleasant circumstances, the doctor may have had a deposition taken of him in connection with another patient's personal injury claim, or a worker's compensation claim, against someone else.

Depositions are taken before a party called a Notary Public, or other person empowered to administer oaths and take testimony. The Notary Public is often a certified court reporter, as well, so that a record of everything said at the deposition can be taken down, and, if it should become necessary, used in court. A formal notice must be given to the party needing to be deposed, and a reasonable time given before the deposition is to be taken. In practice, the attorneys would usually agree, informally, on a time and place (most often the place is in the attorney's office) where the deposition is to be taken.

Generally, the practice is that before the case is heard by the judge or the jury, a deposition will usually be taken of all the parties in the case, as well as others who will likely testify at the trial, including the expert witnesses. True, in some malpractice cases, the attorneys involved in the case may try to make the deposition, ordinarily an informal affair, something of a candid bull session. Nevertheless, if you are the defendant doctor involved in a deposition exercise, please be cautioned of this: do not be fooled. Just know that depositions are an extremely important matter, and should be taken very, very seriously. Why? Because, under the rules, what is said and recorded at a deposition, may be the basis for having the case resolved out of court, without a formal trial. Deposition can also be used to 'impeach' the testimony of the deposed party at trial, and be taken as an admission of some information, among other purposes.

Some pointers on undergoing a deposition.

As a patient, or a doctor, involved in a malpractice case, you'll almost certainly have to have your deposition taken by the opposing attorney. There are a few points you should keep in mind:

- Before the deposition, have a meeting with your attorney to brief you on what to expect.

- Review everything about the case in advance, including any statement you prepared, all your records, the Complaint, and the doctor's answer, answers to the interrogatories, the depositions taken of others, etc. This is a time and place to impress the opposing attorney that you will be a believable witness!

- If you are aware of any discrepancies from the material you have reviewed, discuss how to handle it with your attorney if it should come up.

- Unless the deposition is at your attorney's office, you should meet your attorney at his office and travel together to the place of the deposition.

- When you arrive at the deposition, be courteous but serious. This is not the time to discuss golf scores and tell jokes.

- You should ask your attorney where you should sit.

- When the deposition begins, the Notary Public will ask you to swear that you will tell the truth.

- The doctor's attorney will then proceed to ask you (the patient) questions. You should answer them directly and specifically. However, don't volunteer information. Remain calm. If you don't hear or understand a question, ask that it be repeated or clarified to you.

- While questions are being asked, your attorney may object to some questions. If he does, take his direction as to whether to respond. Don't argue with your attorney. (E.g., don't say to your lawyer, "No, I want to answer that question, when he has said for you not to.") If your attorney objects to a question, the doctor's attorney may, in some cases, ask that the court reporter "certify" the particular question and allow the court to determine whether you must answer it.

- Your (the patient's) attorney may also ask questions. However, he will usually do so only to correct or clarify something that you said. There is no reason to give your attorney more information than requested

- When the deposition is concluded, you may be asked whether you wish to waive the "signing" of the deposition. Your attorney will usually make that decision. When a deposition is taken, you have a right to review it to make certain that it has been properly transcribed. This doesn't give him the right to change answers that you don't like. However, you may clarify answers. The right to sign a deposition is normally waived. If you wish to review it, let your attorney know in advance. The best rule is to not waive signature.

- You may obtain a copy of your deposition. Be certain that you get a copy.

- If you thereafter review the deposition and find a misstatement, let your attorney know. He will know the best way to correct or clarify it.

Depositions are normally taken only for discovery purposes. However, depositions may also be taken for use as evidence at trial. The procedures for taking 'evidence' depositions are somewhat more formal than 'discovery' depositions. This is because an evidence deposition actually can be used as testimony in a trial, if the person deposed is a physician, or is dead or unable to attend the trial. Evidence depositions are seldom taken, unless an important witness is in ill health, or will be unavailable at trial.

3. Inspection of Documents

In connection with interrogatories or depositions, a request is also usually filed, asking to inspect or receive copies of documents, objects, or tangible things, relevant to the case. In medical malpractice cases, of course, your attorney will already have received all hospital and medical records. Thus, the request for document inspection will usually be of greater help to the doctor's attorney, who may request of you (the patient) things such as reports received relative to your injuries.

4. Physical and Mental Examinations

Where a person's physical or mental condition is in issue, as it often would be in a medical malpractice case, discovery rules allow the doctor to obtain, at his own expense, a physical or mental examination of the person. A copy of the examination report must be provided to the person examined. Clearly, if the nature and extent of a patient's injuries are in question, a physical or mental examination is appropriate.

5. Admissions

In order to expedite the trial of a case, a litigant may request another party to either admit a fact, or the genuineness of documents. An admission avoids the need for further evidence on that point. Requests for admissions are particularly helpful in establishing data (e.g., income).

D. THE USE AND VALUE OF EXPERTS

With a few exceptions, generally the determination of the guilt or innocence of the doctor's medical malpractice will depend primarily on what the experts in the field say. Simply summed up, in medical malpractice cases, it is basically the medical experts that will establish the standard of care that applies; hence a patient will usually need an expert's testimony in order to make his case. Thus, to properly pursue or defend a case, each side in the malpractice case must, and usually do, enlist the experts for their testimonies to support his or her position.

Consequently, for an attorney involved in a professional malpractice trial (whether on the side of the plaintiff or the defendant party), the task of getting the right and appropriate experts for the case will be an important and critical task. As fully explained in a previous section of this book (see Chapter IV, Section F thereof), in the modern environment of the practice of malpractice law, this task is hardly a difficult one any more for the vast majority of cases. In fact, in these times, even career professional witnesses, highly qualified physicians and other medical personnel who can be hired and paid to serve as expert witnesses, are commonly available. (For more on this, see Chapter II, Section D (2), and Chapter IV, Section F thereof).

E. SUMMARY JUDGEMENT

The importance of the pretrial skirmishes discussed in this chapter becomes evident when one   realizes that on the basis of them, a judge could 'summarily' (i.e., automatically, with no further evidence taken) rule on a case without a formal trial. The judge would do so by entering "*summary judgment*." A summary judgment is entered when it is clear to the trial judge that (in his or her own judgment so far) one or the other side would most likely win.

To request a summary judgment, an attorney will file a motion with the court. Unless the right to a summary judgment is clear from the complaint and answer, which it seldom is, affidavits or sworn statements will be filed to fill in the facts. Significantly, answers to interrogatories, discovery depositions and admissions of the parties may be used for this purpose as well.

A court will not enter summary judgment if there is some factual dispute, which requires a full hearing in the case. It will do so only if, based on the affidavits filed and the discovery conducted, it seems demonstrated that no material issue of facts remain, but only an issue of how those facts are to be applied.

In medical malpractice cases, it is quite common for the doctor's attorney to file, usually after the depositions and other discovery activities have been undertaken and the lawyer is able to see at that point whether or not the patient has any real case, a motion asking the Judge to issue a Summary Judgment, and the courts to grant them in proper instances in which the doctor has a particularly strong defense basis.

CHAPTER VIII

THE TRIAL

Some Reflections Just Before Trial: Do You Still Wish To Proceed?

All right, let's assume that the day for the trial draws nears. You (the patient) may think that you have already been through the wringer. So has the doctor. As the person who is dragging your doctor to court, you should know this: that the trial will be one of the most emotionally trying times of both of your lives, yours and the doctor's. If you do not prevail, all you will lose is money. As for your doctor, he may not only be required to pay you more than he could earn in a lifetime, but, even more importantly for him, at least, the travail most likely will affect any altruistic inclinations that he previously had, and he may be so emotionally disrupted that he will give up his profession, even though he would ordinarily have probably practiced for another twenty or thirty more years.

As you sit in the courtroom and face the doctor whom you previously trusted with your health and life until he committed "medical malpractice," look him in the eye and ask yourself, "Do I still want to go through with this suit?' You can still call it off.

At some points in the pretrial skirmishes, it's possible you may have had some second thoughts, maybe, about the awful things that your lawyer has vicariously accused the doctor of. But, nevertheless, although you may have liked to call the whole thing off, your lawyer has, in effect, put a gun to your doctor's head and is itching to pull the trigger.

As your doctor sits there, he is asking himself, "How did a trusting patient/doctor relationship deteriorate to this?" He, too, would like to turn back the clock – but he can't. After spending twelve years from the time he graduated from high school in training to learn his skill as a doctor, his entire professional life is now being threatened by this one event. You are accusing him of being a "bad" doctor, probably even a "dangerous" doctor. So, he really has no choice but to make you look as bad as you are trying to make him look. In the mind of every doctor subjected to the ignominious experience of a malpractice trial, he's most likely thinking already, "Win or lose, when this is over, I don't need this, I'm out of the practice of medicine!" If this much does not happen, you can rest assured that, at the very least, this experience will psychologically scar the doctor permanently and severely alter the original sense of idealism and altruistic inclinations of serving humanity that most doctors have when they first leave medical school.

A. GETTING TO COURT

1. Pretrial Conference and Trial Setting

After your doctor has answered your complaint and filed his answer (response) papers with the court, a judge will review the case from time to time with the attorneys on the case to determine if the case is ready for trial. He does this at pretrial conferences. The scheduling of pretrial conferences varies from county to county, or judge to judge. The first conference will usually be scheduled in six months or a year after the answer is filed by your doctor. Thereafter, the conference will be scheduled as agreed by the parties or ordered by the court, depending on the status of the case. If you, the plaintiff, or the doctor (the defendant), want a pretrial conference (and thus a trial) sooner, either one of the attorneys can request a pretrial conference at any time.

At a pretrial conference, the attorneys consider with the court what can be done to expedite the trial. (1) For example, in some cases, a doctor may admit that he is at fault and desires only to contest the amount of the damages, or perhaps the parties might have settled all aspects of the case, except for just one or two of them. The court may also limit the number of expert witnesses which may be called to testify.

2. Final Settlement Efforts

After pretrial the discovery stage is completed, one very useful benefit of that exercise, is that the parties and their attorneys will have a fairly good idea of their respective chances of winning. One side or the other will usually initiate some settlement moves or discussions. Settlement discussions take place well before the pretrial conference. At the pretrial conference, the judge will from time to time be inquiring from the parties whether any settlement efforts have been attempted. If the answer is "Yes," or that settlement is impossible, many judges will usually do little more. When a jury case is involved, other judges do much more, going over the facts and even giving some ideas as to how the case could be settled. An effective judge can do a lot to get the cases which are of the kind that should be settled, settled.

Some Dangers of a 'Quickie' Settlement of a Case For the Doctor

It is usually assumed by many that the first person to blink – to initiate settlement discussions – believes that his case is weak. This is not quite so, however. However, certainly, if the patient's attorney considers his chances of winning slim, he will no doubt bring up making a settlement. Similarly, if the doctor's position is indefensible, or at least shaky, the doctor's carrier may suggest a settlement inasmuch as it would be wise under such circumstances to strike the best possible deal at the lowest possible cost. Many a time, a proposal for settlement is initiated merely because the attorneys are simply realistic about the legal system, particularly the unpredictability of juries. When juries go behind those closed doors, they are "the law." They can decide to throw the patient out of court, or to put the screws on the doctor, or, as they often do, to effect their own settlement of the case.

As a rule, medical malpractice insurance carriers have a habit of preferring to settle cases before they go to trial. They contend that this is less costly, and that an excessive judgment can be avoided. Unfortunately, most insurance policies allow the carrier to settle the cases without the consent of the doctor who is involved in the case.

True, in some instances, making a settlement is appropriate. However, an expedient settlement does nothing to preserve a doctor's reputation as a doctor. Carriers often suggest that a settlement is not a reflection on a doctor's competence, or an admission of guilt, but merely a business decision. This is not quite correct. State law may require that some carriers report the settlement of any claim which alleges medical malpractice to the state licensing board. On the basis of that report, the board may pursue disciplinary action against the doctor. (2) Settlements must also be reported to the National Data Bank. As such, doctors may be reluctant to settle even a deserving case.

3. Other Pretrial Actions

A variety of other pretrial actions may be taken on the eve of trial. They generally serve the purpose of preventing the parties from being surprised at trial by some unanticipated evidence or argument. These are often resolved at the pretrial conference. Some of these actions include the following:

- **Supplemental Interrogatories:** Once the interrogatories questions are asked, the party to whom they are directed has no obligation to update them before the trial, unless he/she is requested to do so. However, a request is often filed to have the interrogatories supplemented.

- **Compelling Attendance of Witnesses:** If there is someone or something (e.g., records) that a party needs at trial to present his case, the party can compel the person he needs, or that has the item, to attend the trial. If the person is not a party to the case, the attorney will subpoena him. If the person is a party, the attorney may simply notify him to appear.

- **Disclosure of Expert you plan to use:** In answer to interrogatories, or at the pretrial conference, you, the patient (plaintiff), will have to disclose the experts you plan to call as witnesses. If this isn't done, some appropriate sanction may be imposed by the judge, like preventing the expert from testifying.

- **Motion in Limine:** Where a case is to be heard by a jury, a party in the case may ask the judge to decide in advance whether some particular evidence can or cannot be presented. This is done by filing what is known as "a motion in limine," meaning one to limit the presentation of evidence. The patient's side will usually try to prevent any evidence that adds to the prestige of the doctor (e.g., that he was the president of the medical staff), or which emotionally supports his position (e.g., he donates hours and hours of service to low-income patients).

In addition to these activities, time will be devoted to making certain that all of the evidence, including the testimony of expert witnesses, is prepared and ready for presentation. The attorney will orchestrate these activities.

4. Some Personal Preparations You Could Use for Trial

You (the patient) will prepare yourself, as does the doctor, for the trial. A very good training on this is this: if at all possible, try to witness an actual medical malpractice trial weeks before your case is heard, either in your own community, or somewhere else in the same state. An ideal situation for you would be for you to observe your own attorney, or even the doctor's attorney, in action at trial. You might be required to travel to another city, but even if that is the case, it would be worth the time and expense in your having a first-hand knowledge of what happens. At a bare minimum, you should insist that your attorney take you to the courthouse and show you where the trial will probably be held. This is so that you become familiar with the physical aspects of the courtroom. Have your attorney show you where all the participants in the case will sit, and explain and demonstrate to you the whole procedures and protocol of a typical medical malpractice trial, as well as your own, specifically.

Your Appearance and Looks At The Trial, Matters To Jurors

PLEASE TAKE GOOD NOTE OF THIS: You should realize that in the trial, no detail should be overlooked. This includes such things as the dress, decorum and body language. Particularly important, is how questions are answered. The jury pays particular attention to appearance, voice, mannerisms and body language of the parties, as well as their witnesses.

Research has shown that in most courtrooms, the jury is favorably impressed if the patient is neatly and conservatively dressed. It is no accident, for example, that the most hardened criminals who are pictured in the newspapers looking disheveled, raunchy, and longhaired characters, appear in court looking completely neat, clean, barbered, and attired in Brooks Brothers suits. Attorneys are conscious of the fact that clothes and personal appearance do help clients win. Things as apparently little as a beard or mustache on the doctor, or on his attorney, in a community which dislikes unshaven men, may affect the jury.

An exception to this rule might be a trial in a depressed, poor area. If the opponent is an appropriately dressed local, and the doctor brings in a flashy attorney with a $200 haircut, adorned with a five karat diamond ring and an alligator briefcase, the jury may be completely turned off regardless of the attorney's ability.

Deciding on the appropriate P.R. techniques should definitely be discussed by the attorneys with their clients, particularly in light of what type of judge and jury are expected to hear the case.

B.   BEGINNING THE TRIAL

1.   Opening Court

At long last the day of the trial arrives. You will meet your attorney at his office and go to the courthouse with him. The doctor will take his files with him when coming to court. At the courthouse, you will follow your attorney's directions. If the case is delayed, a conference room will often be available for you to wait and privately discuss the case with your attorney. Immediately prior to the case beginning, the attorneys will usually meet with the judge to discuss any final procedural matters. Ultimately, the judge will determine that the case is ready to begin and will direct that the parties assemble in the courtroom.

As the case begins, there will be numerous persons in the courtroom. They will include the parties themselves, their attorneys and witnesses, prospective jurors, if this is a jury trial, and the court personnel. The court personnel include a court clerk to maintain the court's records and evidence presented, a court bailiff to maintain order, and a court reporter, to keep a transcript of the hearing unless it is to be tape-recorded. The clerk will then announce the judge's entrance into the courtroom and, out of respect for the court, will direct that those assembled stand while the judge enters. The judge will then ask everyone to be seated.

The judge will first take up some housekeeping tasks. These include such things as stating what the case is, and who the parties are. He will then ask if the parties are present, if they are represented by counsel, and if they are prepared and ready to proceed. Your attorney and the doctor's attorney, will respond, as appropriate. Many times, the judge or the attorneys will make statements, such as "for the record." The record means what is being taken down by the court reporter or the tape. Things which appear quite obvious to those present are not so obvious to another court which might be asked to review the record later.

2.   Picking the Jury

Cases are heard either by a judge, or a judge with a jury. Either party has the right to have a jury trial, and, if they desire a trial by jury, they would have demanded such a trial early in the case. In general, patients request jury trials because juries are more likely to ignore legal technicalities and allow their emotions to justify finding for patients and awarding large judgments. Depending on the disposition of the jury, however, this can backfire and the jurors can see through a patient that's just looking for something for nothing. If a case is to be tried before a jury, the first task in the trial will be to select the members of the jury.

In most states, prospective jurors are randomly selected from among the voters, list of the driver's license holders, or the like. Jurors typically must be residents, adults, and of a fair character. Those randomly selected, are thereafter requested to complete information sheets so that a determination can be made whether they are exempt from serving on a jury, or otherwise not qualified. The names of those remaining are then placed in a box. At a time designated by the judge, the clerk, in the presence of a judge and the county clerk, then draws the names of prospective jurors. These prospective jurors are then required to come to court and may be called as jurors. For that reason, these prospective jurors are sometimes referred to as "venire men" because "*venire*" in Latin means, "to come." (3) From the prospective jurors summoned, the court and the attorneys will proceed with a process known as "impaneling" the jury. This is the process of seating, examining, challenging, passing, and accepting jurors for the case.

The process of impaneling the jury begins by placing the name of each prospective juror into a box, or assigning them numbers placed in a box. In the presence of those assembled for the trial, the names of 12 prospective jurors are selected, and those selected are seated in the jury box. The prospective jurors then undergo what is known as "*voir dire.*" The term literally means, "to speak the truth," and denotes the preliminary examination of prospective jurors to assess their competency, interest, etc. Although practice varies, prospective jurors are examined in panels of four. If one of the four is rejected, another prospective juror from the initial pool is selected. This process goes on until the first panel is complete. Then, the judge and attorneys move to the next panel.

Judges vary on how they handle the voir dire examination of prospective jurors. In general, however, the judge will ask questions. He will then ask questions which the attorney has asked that he pose. Most judges will also allow the attorneys to ask questions directly. To assist in questioning jurors, the judge and attorneys are provided information cards regarding the prospective jurors.

The selection of the jury is one of the most important tasks in the trial of any jury case. This is so important that in recent years there are individuals who do nothing but assist in the selection of jurors. One of the methods used involves defining an ideal juror for a particular case and then trying to assure the selection of 12 "ideal jurors" through the use of psychological considerations, body language, etc. (4)

Challenging The Selection of Jurors You Don't Like

A prospective juror whom you would not like to see included in the jury because, for some reason, you do not think he'll be favorable to your side, can be 'challenged.' There are three types of challenges that can be made:

- **Challenge for Cause:** A prospective juror may be challenged "for cause." This usually involves a juror who has a physical impairment which affects the juror's ability to perceive and appreciate the evidence in the case. Often, jurors are screened in advance so that there are seldom jurors who can be challenged for cause.

- **Challenge for Favor:** A prospective juror may also be challenged for reason of "favor or bias." For example, say the person has in the past been the doctor's patient. Then, that fact, it's reasonable to think and say, is likely to affect his judgment, and so is a proper basis to challenge having him or her picked as a juror. Whether such a juror will actually be excluded from the jury, however, is left up to the discretion of the judge; there is no absolute right to have him or her excluded.

- **Peremptory Challenge:** Each side in a case, is entitled to a number of what is know as "peremptory" type of challenge. These are highly valued and are not used if a prospective juror can be challenged for cause or favor. A peremptory challenge is the right to challenge a juror without having to give any cause or reason for it. Thus, to a limited extent, the doctor has an absolute right to exclude some prospective jurors. An attorney will normally look over the entire group of prospective jurors to avoid wasting peremptory challenges. There may be others that the patient would especially like to be on the jury, but whom the doctor wants to keep off.

Upon completion of the selection of the jury, the jurors, as a group, are sworn to try the issues in the case. The oath will then be administered, by the judge or by the clerk of the court. Thereafter, the judge will often advise the jurors of the importance of their function and thank them for accepting to serve.

3.   The Opening Statements

As soon as the jury is impaneled, the patient's attorney will make an opening statement. The doctor's attorney will usually follow almost immediately, although there are times when the judge would allow the doctor's attorney to give his opening statement at some other time, such as just before the patient's case is presented.

The typical scene in television courtroom dramas (other than The People's Court) portraying the opening statement event, shows a smooth, orderly and overly dramatic scene, the judge presiding, the doctor and his attorney seated at one table, and the accuser and his attorney, at another table, while the jury is in the jury box. Actually, however, the law does not require an opening statement. However, that ritual serves some important purpose in that it provides an opportunity for each attorney to explain in a nutshell his side of the case to the jury. The patient's attorney, by way of the opening statement, will attempt to convince the jury at the very start, that the doctor indeed owed a duty to the patient, and that he breached this duty to the patient by not treating him or her in a manner that conformed with the required standard in its community, that the doctor really injured the patient, and that the doctor was the proximate cause of the patient's injuries. And, therefore, that his client (the patient) is entitled to a lot of money from the doctor. And, on the other hand, the doctor's attorney, in his own opening statement, will, of course, attempt to convince the jury that the doctor, in fact, was not at all negligent.

C.   PRESENTING THE EVIDENCE IN COURT

1. The Plaintiff's (Patient's) Case

Following the opening statements, the patient's attorney will begin to present evidence on the patient's case. At this juncture, the evidence presented by the patient's attorney is called "the patient's case in chief."

What is likely to be the plaintiff's (the patient's) evidence or presentation? Actually, the plaintiff's case, or his witnesses' – what they would probably say at the trial - should come as no surprise to anyone, much less the defendant (the doctor). Certainly not at this stage in the case! More particularly, the doctor (the defense side) should know by now what the patient, or someone else having direct knowledge of the facts of the case, will basically testify, along with the patient's expert witnesses. For one thing, the doctor (the same as his attorney and the entire defense team) has already heard what these persons said in the all-important 'discovery' exercises (Chapter VII, Section C of the book) they had of these persons.

The patient's attorney presents evidence for the plaintiff's side, by "examining" the witnesses and trying to elicit from them any testimony or evidence whatsoever that would suggest or show that the doctor, in his medical treatment of the patient, was in violation of the four basic "elements" involved in a medical malpractice case (Chapter II), more particularly, that he was "negligent" in his medical treatment of the plaintiff, by not providing him the kind of care that was consistent with the standard of care required or expected for treating similar patients in the same or similar community. (The doctor should not forget that he, himself, may even be called to take the stand as an "adverse" or "hostile" witness!) Doctor's attorney may raise objections, and cross-examine the patient.

Throughout the patient's case, the doctor's attorney may make technical objections to the testimony at any time he deems it necessary. He has, as well, the right to "cross-examine" the witnesses, principally the patient and the expert witnesses he presents. He (the doctor's attorney) will basically want to discredit the case presented by the patient and his witnesses; and he will want to set the patient's witnesses up for the evidence that would later be presented on the doctor's behalf. Some dispute matters in the courtroom, are resolved immediately. For example, an objection raised by one attorney or the other, may be "sustained" by the judge, which means that the judge agrees with it, or it may be "overruled," which means that the judge rejects that objection. For other disputes of certain nature, the jurors will be taken out of the courtroom until it is resolved.

At the end of the patient's case, the doctor's attorney will normally request the Judge, almost as a routine matter, that he render a "directed verdict." This is something like a "Summary Judgment," but one that is not granted until after the plaintiff has had the opportunity to present his case and to "give it his best shot." That is, that the Judge, now having heard the patient's actual case, should rule that he has no real or cogent case and therefore enter a judgment in favor of the doctor. It is possible, though quite uncommon, that in a given case, the presiding judge would make such a ruling, taking it upon himself at this stage of the trial, rather than leaving it to the jury, and decide in favor of the doctor right away. This will be done, however, only if a truly frivolous case is involved, especially if there is no jury. Where there is a jury, the judge may have some questions about the case, but will usually prefer to leave it up to the jury.

2. The Defendant's (Doctor's) Case

After the patient's "case in chief" has been presented, then it's the doctor's turn to present his own case and evidence. Basically, the method and procedures used by the defendant, will be similar to that used by the patient in his presentation, as sketched above.

Next, after the doctor has completed his presentation of evidence, the patient's attorney will have another opportunity to make another presentation of evidence. This time, though, evidence or testimony he presents is 'rebuttal' evidence – that is, evidence primarily designed to 'rebut' the doctor's evidence. If the rebuttal evidence is new, the doctor can present evidence to rebut or discredit and cast doubt upon the credibility of the patient's story. In a case heard, not by a jury but by a judge, this part of the trial can go back-and-forth for several times. Judges are not as liberal in jury trials. The patient's attorney will always go last, however, regardless of how many times the parties go back-and-forth. This is so because in a malpractice case such as this, it is the patient that has the burden to prove his case against the doctor.

D. THE FINAL ARGUMENTS

After all evidence has been heard, and all witnesses have been called, each side now presents a final argument. This is basically a summary of the case and what each side believes was proved in the trial.

The patient's attorney will go first. As was the case at the beginning of the case, the patient's attorney will, again, attempt to convince the jury that the evidence showed that the doctor owed a duty to the patient, and that he breached this duty by not treating his client in a manner accepted as the proper standard of care in the community, that the doctor injured the patient, and that the doctor was the proximate cause of his injuries. He will urge the jury to find the doctor guilty of malpractice and suggest that they force the doctor to pay a huge amount of money. On the doctor's part, the doctor's attorney will now attempt to refute the characterizations of the patient's evidence, or the conclusions being drawn from it by the patient's attorney, and would try to convince the jury that the evidence presented goes to show that doctor is, indeed, not guilty of malpractice charges leveled against him. Again, because the patient has the burden of proof to show that the doctor did in fact do what he has been accused of, his (the patient's) attorney will, again, have the last say.

The curtain falls on the last act on the case brought against the doctor!

E. JURY INSTRUCTIONS BY THE JUDGE

If this is a case that had been heard by a jury, the judge will instruct the jury – it's also called "charging the jury" - as to the law of the rules to be applied in the case. While a jury determines "the facts" of the case, the judge determines "the law," that is, the rules by which those facts are to be applied or judged. The judge instructs the jury on the law or rules, by way of the "jury instructions" he reads the jurors after the final arguments are concluded.

Prior to the trial reaching this stage, the judge will have directed the attorneys to prepare their own "suggested instructions." These instructions are to be simple, brief, impartial, and free from argument. The judge will then determine which of these instructions to present to the jury.

The instructions will begin with some general cautionary instructions. Jurors are told, for example, that neither sympathy nor prejudice should influence them in their determinations or judgment, and that they are to consider ONLY the testimony of the witnesses and the exhibits offered and received in the court records. (5) Various other instructions are given, including those pertaining to evaluation of the evidence, determining what constitutes 'negligence,' and establishing damages. Of particular interest, are those instructions specifically pertaining to malpractice. A review of these will give some idea of how the law is presented to the jury. These instructions would, as appropriate, be given along with other instructions applicable to the case.

Sample of Jury Instructions On Doctor's Duty & Negligence

Throughout this book, reference has been made, again and again, to the 'duty' of a doctor to his/her patient. (6) A trial judge's instructions given in a malpractice case, may describe that duty as follows:

In [treating] [operating upon] a patient, a [doctor] [dentist] must possess and apply the knowledge, and use the skill and care, that is ordinarily used by reasonably well-qualified [doctors] [dentists] in the locality in which he practices or in similar localities in similar cases and circumstances. A failure to do so is a form of negligence that is called malpractice.

[The only way in which you may decide whether the defendant possessed and applied the knowledge and used the skill and care which the law required of him, is from the evidence that had been presented in this trial by {doctors} {dentists} called as expert witnesses. You must not attempt to determine this question from any personal knowledge you have.] (7)

If a specialist is involved, his duty is described in this manner:

In [treating] [operating upon] a patient, a [doctor] [dentist] who holds himself out as a specialist and undertakes service in a particular branch of medical, surgical, or other healing science, must possess and apply the knowledge, and use the skill and care, which reasonably well-qualified specialists in the same field, practicing in the same locality, or in similar localities, ordinarily would use in similar cases and circumstances. A failure to do so is a form of negligence called malpractice. (8)

Sample of Jury Instructions On failure by Doctor to Refer a Patient

Where the complaint alleges that a doctor failed to refer a patient to a specialist, the instruction given could read:

If, in the treatment of a patient, a [doctor] [dentist] realizes, or, if, in the exercise of that care and skill which a reasonably well-qualified [doctor] [dentist] would ordinarily use in the locality in which he practices, or in similar localities, should realize that the nature of the patient's illness [condition] requires the services of a [physician] [surgeon] [dentist] skilled in a special branch of [medical] [surgical] [dental] science, then the [doctor] [dentist] is under a duty to [advise the patient to consult a specialist] [refer the patient to a specialist]. (9)

Sample of Jury Instructions On a Doctor Liable for the Negligence of Someone else (i.e., a surgical nurse)

Where an effort is made to hold a doctor liable for the negligence of someone else, such as a surgical nurse, (10) his responsibility could be described as follows:

When it is customary in similar cases and circumstances for reasonably well-qualified [doctors] [dentists] to delegate the work, such as the work of (e.g., sponge counting to, say a nurse), then the [doctor] [dentist] may delegate that work to a (nurse) and, if he does so, he is not then responsible for the acts or omissions of the nurse to whom the work of sponge counting was delegated. If, however, the defendant knew, or in the exercise of ordinary care should have known, that the nurse was negligently performing or omitting to perform the work, it was the duty of the defendant to take reasonable care to see that the work of sponge counting was done properly. (11)

Sample of Jury Instructions On failure of a Doctor to Obtain Proper Consent

Where it is claimed that the doctor did not obtain any consent for the treatment, (12) the judge's jury instruction could be:

[However, (if the patient is a minor) (if the patient is not in possession of his faculties) (when obtaining consent from the patient would endanger his health), then the surgeon is excused from obtaining the consent of the patient in the operation. In that event, he must obtain consent from a person authorized to consent to the operation (unless it is impracticable to obtain consent because of an emergency or because the delay would endanger the patient's health)] (13)

Sample of Jury Instructions On failure of a Doctor to Obtain Proper Consent in Emergency Situations

Special instructions regarding consent are prescribed if treatment was provided in an emergency arising either before or during an operation. Before an operation, the instruction would state:

Ordinarily a [surgeon] must obtain the consent of a patient before operating on him. However, if an emergency arises that requires treatment in order to protect the patient's health and it is impossible or impracticable to obtain consent either from the patient or someone authorized to consent for him, a [surgeon] may undertake treatment, provided that what he does is within the customary practice of reasonably well qualified [surgeons] practicing in the same or similar localities in similar cases and circumstances. (14)

And if the emergency arises during an operation, the instruction would provide:

Ordinarily a [surgeon] must obtain consent of the patient for a specific operation. However, if, during the course of an operation for which consent has been obtained, an emergency arises requiring further or different treatment to protect the patient's health, and it is impossible or impracticable to obtain consent either from the patient or from someone authorized to consent for him, the surgeon must give the further or different treatment required, provided that what he does is within the customary practice of reasonable well-qualified [surgeons] practicing in the same or similar localities in similar cases and circumstances. (15)

Sample of Jury Instructions On failure of Patient to Follow Doctor's Instructions

If a doctor is defending a case on the basis that the patient failed to follow the doctor's instructions or refused treatment, the following instruction will be given:

A patient is required to follow reasonable advice as to treatment. In addition, he must follow the doctor's [postoperative treatment] [instructions]. A doctor is not liable for the consequences of a patient's failure to do so. [A patient's failure to receive treatment or follow instructions does not absolve the doctor from the results of any earlier malpractice. It only absolves him from any injury caused by the patient's not accepting reasonable treatment or following instructions. (16)

THE JURY DELIBERATIONS: What follows after the judge's instructions to the jury?

After the jury is instructed on the law and rules to be applied, the judge directs that the bailiff take the jurors to a private room – the jury room – where they will deliberate in private until they reach a decision in the case.

F. THE VERDICT

Because the jury's deliberations are held in secret, there is little to dictate just how jurors proceed in reaching a decision in a case. However, the most common practice is for jurors to select one person from their number to serve as their 'foreman' to preside over the jury's deliberations. Under the foreman's directions, the jurors quickly get down to business and reach a decision.

The decision reached is called a "verdict." Once it is reached, the judge is informed by the jury foreman and the parties to the case are called into the courtroom. The parties, again, assemble in the courtroom, with the judge presiding and the jury seated. The verdict is then announced to the parties, usually by the foreman of the jury.

In almost every state, the jury's verdict must be unanimous. In the event that there is any doubt in a given case, that the decision presented is in fact the decision of ALL the jurors, each may be polled and asked in the open court whether he or she joins in the verdict. On the other hand, where a jury is unable to reach a unanimous decision, it is said that there is a "hung jury," and a new trial may be held. In civil cases, there rarely is a hung jury because, if nothing else, the jurors would usually haggle among themselves until they reach a "settlement" of one kind for the litigants.

After the verdict is returned, the court will enter a "judgment" in the case. The JUDGMENT is the formal, final conclusion of the trial.

G.   POST-TRIAL ACTIVITIES

1.   Post-Trial Motions

After the trial is concluded, a party can file a post-trial motion. The purpose of this action, is to ask the judge to throw out the jury's decision because of some technicality. A similar motion can be filed in cases where the judge hears the case without a jury. The judge will consider the motion and enter an appropriate order which could even include ordering an entirely new trial.

2.   Appeal

In lieu of, or in addition to, a post-trial motion, the judgment can be appealed. There is a right to appeal the case to the appellate court. After the appeal is considered by the appellate court and it renders its own verdict, the State's Supreme Court (the next and highest court in the State) has the legal discretion either to consider or not to consider the appeal - if the appellate court's verdict were to be appealed to the state Supreme Court. (17)

If the doctor wins the case, the patient may threaten or even file an appeal. This could well be a ploy to get some settlement of the case and stave off a suit for malicious prosecution. In such a situation, however, you can bet your life that, on the doctor's part, after what he has gone through already, he doesn't want to give the plaintiff even a cent! Most likely, the doctor will take his chances with the appeal because once a judge, and especially a jury, has ruled against the patient in a case, it's unlikely that the decision will be reversed on appeal.

If it is the patient that wins the case, the doctor will usually consider, with his attorney advising, whether to appeal that decision. A significant percentage of judgments against doctors are reversed on appeal, primarily because the appeal court deems that the expert testimony presented by the patient was not adequate. If there is a sound technical basis for the appeal, the doctor should do so. In some cases, the doctor might consider an appeal as his own ploy to negotiate downward the damages awarded.

IN THE CIRCUIT COURT OF THE EIGHTH JUDICIAL CIRCUIT OF ILLINOIS, ADAMS COUNTY

ANSWER TO THE COMPLAINT

Patient Mary Doe; Patient Agnes Doe,

(Plaintiffs,)

v.

No._____

XYZ Hospital; Dr. Malpractice Davidson

Glen & Hultz
Clerk Circuit Court 8th Judicial Circuit
ILLINOIS, ADAMS CO.

(Defendants.)

93

Defendant's <u>ANSWER TO COMPLAINT</u>

<u>COUNT ONE</u>

NOW come the Defendants, XYZ Hospital and Dr. Malpractice Davidson, by their attorneys, James E. Defense, Esq., and for their answer to Count One of Plaintiffs' Complaint at Law, state as follows:

1. That Defendants admit the allegations contained in paragraph 1 of Count One.
2. That Defendants admit the allegations contained in paragraph 2 of Count One.
3. That Defendants admit the allegations contained in paragraph 3 of Count One.
4. That Defendants admit the allegations contained in paragraph 4 of Count One.
5. That Defendants admit the allegations contained in paragraph 5 of Count One.
6. That Defendants admit the allegations contained in paragraph 6 of Count One.
7. That Defendants admit the allegations contained in paragraph 7 of Count One.
8. That Defendants admit the allegations contained in paragraph 8 of Count One.
9. That Defendants deny each and every allegation contained in paragraph 9 of Count One, including sub-paragraphs a, b, c, d, e, f and g, contained therein.
10. That Defendants deny the allegations contained in paragraph 10 of Count One.
11. That Defendants admit the Plaintiffs attached an affidavit and report but deny the remaining allegations contained in paragraph 11 of Count One.

WHEREFORE, Defendants, XYZ Hospital and Dr. Malpractice Davidson, deny that the Plaintiffs are entitled to judgment in any sum whatsoever and pray that said cause of action be dismissed.

COUNT TWO

Now come the Defendants, XYZ Hospital and Dr. Malpractice Davidson, by their attorneys, James E. Defense, Esq., and for their answer to Count Two of Plaintiffs' Complaint at Law, state as follows:

1. That Defendants admit the allegations contained in paragraph 1 of Count Two.
2. That Defendants admit the allegations contained in paragraph 2 of Count Two.
3. That Defendants admit the allegations contained in paragraph 3 of Count Two.
4. That Defendants admit the allegations contained hi paragraph 4 of Count Two.
5. That Defendants admit the allegations contained in paragraph 5 of Count Two.
6. That Defendants admit the allegations contained in paragraph 6 of Count Two.
7. That Defendants admit the allegations contained in paragraph 7 of Count Two.
8. That Defendants admit the allegations contained in paragraph 8 of Count Two.
9. That Defendants deny each and every allegation contained in paragraph 9 of Count Two, including sub-paragraphs a, b, c, d, e, f and g contained therein.
10. That Defendants deny the allegations contained in paragraph 10 of Count Two.
11. That Defendants lack sufficient knowledge of the allegations contained in paragraph 11 of Count Two and, therefore, deny said allegations.

WHEREFORE, Defendants Dr. Malpractice Davidson, and XYZ Hospital, an Illinois corporation, deny that the Plaintiffs are entitled to judgment in any sum whatsoever and pray that the said cause of action be dismissed.

SIGNED: James E. Defense, Esq.
Attorney for Defendant

AUTHORIZATION For Release of Medical Information
(Sample)

Name of Patient: _____   Medical Record No: _____

Date of Request: _____ Date Needed: _____   Date of Birth: _____

I authorize the use or disclosure of the above named individual's health information , its employees and agents, to furnish:

FROM: TO:

Name: _____   Name: _____

Address: _____   Address: _____

_____   _____

Telephone: _____ Fax: _____   Telephone: _____ Fax: _____

The type of information to be used or disclosed is as follows (check all of the appropriate boxes and details as needed):

Dates of Service/Treatment: _____

- [ ] Discharge Summary
- [ ] History and Physical
- [ ] Consultations
- [ ] Operative Reports
- [ ] Emergency Department Records
- [ ] Laboratory and Pathology Reports
- [ ] Entire Record for dates of service
- [ ] Other (please specify): _____

- [ ] Cardiology Reports (EKG, ECHO, Cath, etc)
- [ ] Therapy Notes (PT, ST, OT, Radiation, etc)
- [ ] Clinic Notes (Wound, Pain, Physician, etc)
- [ ] Mental Health Records
- [ ] X-ray Reports
- [ ] X-ray Films
- [ ] Billing Statements

I understand that the information in my health record may include information relating to sexually transmitted disease, acquired immunodeficiency syndrome (AIDS), or human immunodeficiency virus (HIV). It may also include information about behavioral or mental health services, and treatment for alcohol and drug abuse. A request in writing must be made to exclude the above from the disclosed information.

The purpose for which this disclosure is being made is:
- [ ] My personal records
- [ ] Sharing with other healthcare providers
- [ ] Other (please describe) _____

I understand that I have the right to revoke this Authorization at any time. I understand that if I revoke this authorization, I must do so in writing and present my written revocation to the health information management department. I understand that the revocation will not apply information that has already been released in response to this authorization.

I understand that once the above information is disclosed, it may be redisclosed by the recipient and the information may not be protected by federal privacy laws or regulations. I understand that I have the right to inspect and copy the information that is to be disclosed.

This Authorization expires on: _____. If I fail to specify an expiration date, this authorization will expire six months from date of signature.

I understand authorizing the use or disclosure of the information identified above is voluntary. Healthcare treatment, payment, enrollment in the health plan, or eligibility for benefits is not conditioned on signing the authorization.

_____   _____   _____   _____
Witness   Date   Signature of Patient or Legal Representative   Date

Legal Representative Relationship (POA) _____

This Authorization must be signed by the patient or guardian if patient is less than 18. If the patient is a minor, and the records deal with mental health treatment, alcohol or drug abuse, or venereal disease, this Authorization must be signed by the minor. If the patient is mentally incompetent to sign this Authorization, it must be signed by the appropriate legal representative of the patient.

CHAPTER IX

ARE THERE LEGITIMATE INSTANCES WHEN ONE'S DOCTOR SHOULD RIGHTLY BE SUED?

A. TO SUE YOUR DOCTOR, IS IT EVER RIGHT?

QUESTION: are there good, legitimate occasions and circumstances when a patient not only may, but, in fact, should even be obligated even if as a civic duty to society, to sue his/her doctor for malpractice? Absolutely! However, in the ultimate interest of that same society, and the long-term survivability of that same society and what is probably its most vital life-sustaining institutions, it is imperative that patients be absolutely certain that they have precisely that kind of a situation, before they rush to court for such legal "remedy." Or, perhaps more accurately, before they allow themselves to be stampeded into running to the courts by rapacious trial lawyers who dominate the increasingly lucrative American medical malpractice industry! In the final analysis, the critical point for the patient, for America today, is this: is this current courtroom "remedy" really the permanent, sustainable, workable solution to the American health care crisis? Has it brought the patient any closer to relief for their primary need and interest in health care – improvement in the quality of health care for them? That is, could we be throwing out the baby (the entire health care system, which we all profess to desire), with the bath water (a few dollars for a handful of patients, and lots of it for the greedy lawyers)?

To be sure, there is a growing perception among many in America that some doctors today, despite their high training and impressive credentials, are greedy money grabbers and arrogant S.O.B's. These aberrant ones, it is true, give the profession a bad name. There is, in addition, the disturbing danger that the truly bad mal-practitioners, the worst of the worst, among the American doctors, could get even more clever and expert at avoiding getting sued, but the dedicated, well-intentioned, honest doctors with less expertise at avoidance of getting sued, will take the brunt of getting "nailed." And we, Americans, lose the good doctors and are stuck with the fumbler.

This book is not intended to imply that all or most medical malpractice suits are frivolous. The right legally to seek redress by truly injured patients should be preserved. There are good, bad and careless physicians. And those that fail the Oath of Hippocrates should be dispatched with aplomb from the continued practice of medicine.

B. SOME SUGGESTED REFORMS FOR THE PRESENT SYSTEM & REAL REMEDIES FOR THE PATIENT

In the view of the author, a career medical doctor with real personal and family interest, as well, in the well-being of the lawyers and the legal profession, and, of course, of the medical patients, a more desirable but viable alternate to the current medical malpractice crisis, would be a reformation of the legal system that puts a cap on awards and replaces the excessive money "awards" with a system that shuts down the incompetents with suspension and revocation of licensure. Even killing all the lawyers would not solve all of the problems confronting the current dysfunctional health care delivery system of our nation. For, if you consider the person (your doctor), who you say has done all these awful things to you and your life, to be really as bad and terrible as your lawyer's Complaint says he is, then you should want to put that 'terrible' person out of business! Instead of demanding tons of money award as your 'remedy,' why not seek to petition the State officials to take away that doctor's license to practice so that he cannot injure you or anyone else ever?

C. THE PRIMARY ROOT CAUSES OF THE AMERICAN HEALTH CRISIS

A simplistic explanation of the core problem, suggests that the system has become too sophisticated, too fragmented, too innovative, and certainly too expensive. All of this has happened faster than the American economy can pay for all of the wonderful inventions that the entrepreneurial hospital and health care engineers, health researchers, drug companies, and medical trainers and researchers, are turning out at a frenetic pace.

The voracious American information industry and news media that's always in search of a sensational story, grabs upon any new and innovative health care idea that happens, while anyone who perceives a personal benefit almost immediately demands as a right an immediate access to the latest technology, regardless of cost. Not too long ago, for example, at the Cook County Hospital in Chicago, arthritis was a vexatious problem that confined thousands of patients to wheelchairs. Salicylates, such as aspirin, were the only minimally effective therapy for it. Dosage was limited by the frequent complication of gastrointestinal problems that included uncontrollable bleeding ulcers. Hoping to increase the dose by administering salicylates intravenously and thus bypassing the stomach, a County staff doctor asked one of the well-known pharmaceutical manufacturers to prepare a solution that could be administered by vein. This was accomplished. But then, thanks largely to a piece in the Reader's Digest by Paul DeKruif, a popular writer on medical subjects, extolling the 'new' and 'sensational' therapy, hundreds of letters, calls, political pressures, and even threats, poured in from everywhere, from not only all across the United States, but the foreign countries, demanding immediate access to the supposedly 'new' medicine! Repeated explanations that this was only an old, pre-existing drug to which all persons already had access, and that the only innovation about it was that it was given intravenously, did nothing to calm the popular uproar!

Not much has changed in America in this regard since those days! It does not matter that the cost is absolutely prohibitive, and the long-term value unproven, patients with liver disease today, are demanding that baboons give up their livers for human transplantation. It may be distasteful all right to American consumers of the American health care delivery system. Nevertheless, Americans must begin to be told, that, realistically, possible rationing will need to be addressed in America, just as it has been done in other countries that have adopted a national health care system.

Another medical misconception today, is the belief that there are not enough "doctors" in America. Not so! Actually, there are too many doctors, except that it is of the wrong kind, of the wrong kinds of medical "specialists." The doctors we have around currently (a good deal of them, at least) are specialists, health care providers, who know more and more about less and less. Prior to World War II, the majority of doctors were general practitioners, broadly trained and able to care for 95% of medical-surgical problems. Then, during World War II, the military gave preference to specialization. As a result, in the postwar period, there was a mad rush to create and enroll in specialty and subspecialty training programs.

Today, however, some 50 or 60 years later, this "over-specialization" craze has had one major detrimental result, among many possible others. Thus, today we find that although it would seem logical that a physician should approach an ailing human in a holistic, 'whole person' manner, the multitude of specialties pursue a disease from strictured agendas, seeming oblivious to the fact that an integrated knowledge of the whole person, is necessary to understand the parts. A serious defect of overspecialization is the compulsion of specialists to create monopolistic barriers against broadly based health care providers. It is primarily this segmentation by unnecessary specialization, that is running up the cost of medical and surgical care.

How and where will all this end? Well, no one really knows! What we do know, however, is that the most 'efficient,' but brutal and undesirable form of management, is a dictatorship. As a society, if we continue in America as we are going, we will wind up with a national health care controlled by an ultimate government dictator. In the process, you, the patient, will be left with no choice but probably to lose your right completely to sue your doctor for medical malpractice, among other vital rights that are traditionally deemed the natural rights of being "American"!

Sample, STANDARD INTERROGATORIES UNDER ILLINOIS SUPREME COURT RULE

Medical Malpractice - to the Defendant (the Doctor)

1. State your full name, professional and residence addresses, and attach a current copy of your curriculum vitae (CV). In the event you do not have a CV, state in detail your professional qualifications, including your education by identifying schools from which you graduated and the degrees granted and dates thereof, your medical internships and residencies, fellowships and a bibliography of your professional writing(s).

2. State whether you have held any position on a committee or with an administrative body at any hospital. If so, state when you held such position(s) and the duties and responsibilities involved in such position(s).

3. Have you ever been named as a defendant in a lawsuit arising from alleged malpractice or professional negligence? If so, state the court, the caption and the case number for each lawsuit.

4. Since the institution of this action, have you been asked to appear before or attend any meeting of a medical committee or official board of any medical society or other entity for the purpose of discussing this case? If so, state the date(s) of each such meeting and the name and address of the committee, society or other entity conducting each meeting.

5. Have you ever testified in court in a medical malpractice case? If so, state the court, the caption and the case number of each such case, the approximate date of your testimony, whether you testified as a treating physician or expert and whether you testified on your own behalf or on behalf of the defendant or the plaintiff.

6. Has your license to practice medicine ever been suspended or has any disciplinary action ever been taken against you in reference to your license? If so, state the specific disciplinary action taken, the date of the disciplinary action, the reason for the disciplinary action, the period of time for which the disciplinary action was effective and the name and address of the disciplinary entity taking the action.

7. State the exact dates and places on and at which you saw the plaintiff for the purpose of providing care or treatment.

8. State the name, author, publisher, title, date of publication and specific provision of all medical texts, books, journals or other medical literature which you or your attorney intend to use as authority or reference in defending any of the allegations set forth in the complaint.

9. Were you named or covered under any policy or policies of liability insurance at the time of the care and treatment alleged in the complaint? If so, state for each policy:

    a. The name of the insurance company;

    b. The policy number;

c. The effective policy period;

d. The maximum liability limits for each person and each occurrence, including umbrella and excess liability coverage; and

e. The named insured(s) under the policy.

10. Are you incorporated as a professional corporation? If so, state the legal name of your corporation and the name(s) and address(es) for all shareholders.

11. If you are not incorporated as a professional corporation, state whether you were affiliated with a corporate medical practice or partnership in any manner on the date of the occurrence alleged in the complaint. If so, state the name of the corporate medical practice or partnership, the nature of your affiliation and the dates of your affiliation.

12. Were you at any time an employee, agent, servant, shareholder or partner of [NAME OF HOSPITAL]? If so, state the date(s) and nature of your relationship.

13. State whether there were any policies, procedures, guidelines, rules or protocols for [THE PROCEDURE COMPLAINED OF] that were in effect at [NAME OF THE HOSPITAL WHERE PROCEDURE WAS PERFORMED] at the time of the care and/or treatment alleged in the complaint. If so, state:

a. Whether such policies, guidelines, rules or protocols are published and by whom;

b. The effective date of said policies, guidelines, rules or protocols;

c. Which medical professionals are bound by said policies, guidelines, rules or protocols;

d. Who is the administrator of any such policies, procedures, guidelines, rules and/or protocols; and

e. Whether the policies, guidelines, rules or protocols in effect at the time of the occurrence alleged in the complaint have been changed, amended, or altered since the occurrence. If so, state the change(s) and the date(s) of any such change(s).

14. Were any photographs, movies and/or videotapes taken of the plaintiff or of the procedures complained of? If so, state the date(s) on which such photographs, movies and/or videotapes were taken, who is displayed therein, who now has custody of them, and the name, address, occupation and employer of the person taking them.

15. Do you know of any statements made by any person relating to the care and treatment or the damages described in the complaint? If so, give the name and address of each such witness and

the date of the statement, and state whether such statement was written or oral and if written the present location of each such statement.

16. Do you have any information:

a. That any plaintiff was, within the 10 years immediately prior to the care and treatment described in the complaint, confined in a hospital and/or clinic, treated by a physician and/or other health professional, or x-rayed for any reason other than personal injury? If so, state the name of each plaintiff so involved, the name and address of each such hospital and/or clinic, physician, technician and/or health-care professional, the approximate date of such confinement or service and state the reason for such confinement or service.

b. That any plaintiff has suffered any serious personal injury and/or illness within 10 years prior to the date of the occurrence? If so, state the name of each plaintiff so involved and state when, where and how he or she was injured and/or ill and describe the injuries and/or illness suffered.

c. That any plaintiff has suffered any serious personal injury and/or illness since the date of the occurrence? If so, state the name of each plaintiff so involved and state when, where and how he or she was injured and/or ill and describe the injuries and/or illness suffered.

d. That any other suits have been filed for any plaintiff's personal injuries? If so, state the name of each plaintiff involved, the nature of the injuries claimed, the court(s) and caption(s) in which filed, the year(s) filed, and the title(s) and docket number(s) of the suit(s).

e. That any claim for workers' compensation benefits has been filed for any plaintiff? If so, state the name and address of the employer, the date(s) of the accident(s), the identity of the insurance company that paid any such benefits and the case number(s) and jurisdiction(s) where filed.

17. Have you (or has anyone acting on your behalf) had any conversations with any person at any time with regard to the manner in which the care and treatment described in the complaint was provided, or have you overheard any statement made by any person at any time with regard to the injuries complained of by the plaintiff or the manner in which the care and treatment described in the complaint was provided? If so, state the following:

a. The date or dates of such conversation(s) and/or statement(s);

b. The place of such conversation(s) and/or statements(s);

c. All persons present for the conversation(s) and/or statement(s);

d. The matters and things stated by the person in the conversation(s) and/or statement(s);

e. Whether the conversation(s) was oral, written and/or recorded; and

102

f. Who has possession of the statement(s) if written and/or recorded.

18. Pursuant to *Illinois Supreme Court Rule 213(f)*, provide the name and address of each witness who will testify at trial and all other information required for each witness.

19. Identify any statements, information and/or documents known to you and requested by any of the foregoing interrogatories which you claim to be work product or subject to any common law or statutory privilege, and with respect to each interrogatory, specify the legal basis for the claim as required by *Illinois Supreme Court Rule 201(n)*.

20. List the names and addresses of all persons (other than yourself and persons heretofore listed) who have knowledge of the facts regarding the care and treatment complained of in the complaint filed herein and/or of the injuries claimed to have resulted therefrom.

ATTESTATION

STATE OF ILLINOIS   )
)SS.
COUNTY OF   )

       , being first duly sworn on oath, deposes and states that he/she is a defendant in the above-captioned matter, that he/she has read the foregoing document, and the answers made herein are true, correct and complete to the best of his/her knowledge and belief.

_____
SIGNATURE

SUBSCRIBED and SWORN to before me this   day of   , 2XXX

_____
NOTARY PUBLIC

APPENDIX A

SOME BIBLIOGRAPHY

References and Sources Cited in the Book

NOTE: Illinois law has largely been cited in the book as the primary resources. However, it should be noted that the rules stated in the book, generally apply to most states. The citations listed are numbered under each Chapter in the book.

Chapter II
1. W. Keeton, Prosser and Keeton on The Law of Torts at 2 (5th ed. 1984).
2. Id. at 5-6.
3. Id. at 160.
4. Bartimus v. Paxton Community Hospital, 120 Ill. App.2d 1060, 458 N.E.2d 1072, 76 Ill. Dec.418 (1954).
5. Id.
6. Id.
7. Id.
8. Thompson v. Webb.---Ill. App. 3d—, 486 N.E.2d 326, 93 Ill Dec. 225 (1985).
9. Id.
10. Jury instructions are discussed in Chapter VIII, Section E..
11. Illinois Pattern Jury Instructions - Civil s 105.01.
12. Illinois Pattern Jury Instructions -Civil s 105.02.
13. Metz v. Fairbury Hospital. 118 Ill. App. 3d 1093, 455 N.E.2d 1096. 74 Ill. Dec. 472 (1983).
14. Spike v. Sellett. 102 Ill. App. 3d 270, 430 N.E.2d 597, 58 Ill. Dec. 565 (1981).
15. Borowski v. Von Solbrig, 60 Ill. 2d 418, 328 N.E.2d 301 (1975).

Chapter III
1. Adapted from Pratt v. Davis, 224 Ill. 300, 79 N.E. 562 (1906).
2. Illinois Pattern Jury Instructions s 105.07.
3. W. Keeton, Prosser and Keeton on The Law of Torts at 190 (5th ed. 1984).
4. Id. at 189-190.
5. Green v. Hussey,' 127 Ill. App. 2d 174, 262 N.E.2d 156 (1970); Ohligschlager v. Procter Community Hospital, 6 Ill. App. 3d 81, 282 N.E.2d 86 (1972); Casey v. Penn, 45 Ill. App. 3d 1068, 362 N.E.2d 1973, 6 Ill. Dec. 453 (1977) S.. Guebard v. Jabaay, 117 Ill. App. 1.452 N.E.2d 751, 72 Ill. Dec. 498 (1983).
7. Miceikis v. Field, 37 Ill. App.3d 763, 347 N.E.2d 320 (1976).
8. Id. 347 N.E.2d at 324.
9. See Riskin. Informed Consent; Looking for the Action. 1975 University of Illinois Law Forum 580.
10. Id.
11. 410 Illinois Compiled Statutes 201/1.

12. 755 Illinois Compiled Statutes 5/11-1.
13. See Illinois Compiled Statutes 201/1.
14. Illinois Compiled Statutes 201/1.
15. 755 Illinois Compiled Statutes 5/11/7.
16. 410 Illinois Compiled Statutes 210/2.
17. Although the term "divorce" is used, the term currently in local vogue is "dissolution of marriage."
18. 750 Illinois Compiled Statutes 5/608.
19. 750 Illinois Compiled Statutes 5/602-1.
20. 755 Illinois Compiled Statutes 5/11-13.
21. 755 Illinois Compiled Statutes 5/11-13.
22. 410 Illinois Compiled Statutes 210/3.
23. Leno v. St. Joseph Hospital. 55 1 1 1 . 2d 114. 302 N.E. 2d 58 (1973).
24. See Id.
25. See below.
26. See Leno v. St. Joseph Hospital, 55 I I I . 2d 114, 3O2 N.E.2d 58 (1973).
27. 755 Illinois Compiled Statutes 630/1. et seg.
28. 755 Illinois Compiled Statutes 630/3 and 630/4.
29. 755 Illinois Compiled Statutes 630/3.
30. 755 Illinois Compiled Statutes 5O/5.
31. Id.
32. 755 Illinois Compiled Statutes 50/7.
33. 755 Illinois Compiled Statutes 50/3..
34. Id.
35. Id.
36. See, e.g., Schaecher v. Reinwein, 41 1 1 1 . App. 3d 1O55, 355 N.E.2d 351 (1976)
37. This is a condition where the umbilical cord becomes compressed between the baby and the mother's pelvis.
38. Adapted from Jones v. Karraker, 109 1 1 1 . App. 3d 363, 440 N.E.2d 420, 64 1 1 1 . Dec. 868 (1982) The judgment was for *125,000.
39. These general concepts were discussed in an earlier chapter.
40. Spike v. Sellett, 102 1 1 1 . App. 3d 270, 430 N.E. 2d 597, 58 1 1 1 . Dec/ 565 (1981).
41. Wise v. St. Mary's Hospital, 64 1 1 1 . App. 3d 587, 381 N.E. 2d 809, 21 1 1 1 . Dec. 482 (1978).
42. Spike v. Sellett, 102 1 1 1 . App. 3d 270, 430 N.E. 2d 597, 58 1 1 1 . Dec. 565 (1981).
43. By this method,' the doctor places two fingers in the baby's mouth in order to lower the chin and supports the baby's body with either his forearm or with the assistance of a towel around the baby.
44. It was also suggested that the cervix could have been cut (Duhrssen incision), but that this is difficult to do, is not a common procedure and is considered by some doctors to be obsolete.
45. Adapted from Carman v. Dippold, 63 1 1 1 . App. 3d 419, 379 N.D. 2d 1365, 20 1 1 1 . Dec. 297 (1978).
46. Cirafici v. Goffen, 85 1 1 1 . App. 3d 1102, 407 N.E.2d 633. 41 1 1 1 . Dec. 135 (1980).
47. See Cirafici v. Goffen, 85 1 1 1 . App. 3d 1102, 407 N.E.2d 633 41 1 1 1 . Dec. 135 (1980). The court in this case noted that other reasons include that: such contracts may retard the advancement of medical science and would thereby be contrary to public policy; they would cause physicians to practice defensive medicine: and the physician's statements, being merely expressions of opinions, prediction, or optimistic prognostications of probable results should not be actionably.
48. Guilmet v. Campbell, 385 Mich. 57, 188 N.W. 2d 601 (1971).
49. Hawkins v. McGee, 84 N.H. 114, 146 A. 641 (1929).
50. Robins v. Finestone, 308 N.Y. 543, 127 N.E.2d 330 (1959).
51. Noel v. Proud, 189 Kan. 6, 367 P.2d 61 (1961).
52. Crawford v. Duncan, 61 Cal. App. 647. 215 P. 573 (1923).

53. Bailey v. Harmon, 74 Colo. 390, 222 P. 393 (1924).

54. Camposano v. Claiborn, 2 Conn. Cir. 135, 196 A. 2d 129.

55. Sullivan v. O'Connor, 363 Mass. 579, 296 N.E.2d 182 (1973).

56. Adapted from Cirafici v. Goffen, 85 Ill. App. 2d 1102, 407 N.E. 2d 633, 41 Ill. Dec. 135 (1980). The court did not decide the merits of the case could be heard.

57. Siemienic v. Luthern General Hospital, 134 Ill. App. 3d 823, 480 N.E. 2d 1227, 89 Ill. Dec. 484 (1985).

58. Id.

59. Id.

60. Cockrum v. Baumgartner, 95 Ill.2d 193, 447 N.E. 2d 385, 69 Ill. Dev. 168 (1983).

61. Id.

62. Id. 69 Ill. Dec. at 172

63. Wilczynski v. Goodman, 73 Ill. App. 3d 51, 62, 391 N.E. 2d 479, 29 Ill. Dec. 216 (1979).

64. Adapted from Cockrum V. Baumgartner, 95 Ill. 2d 193, 447 N.E. 2d 385, 69 Ill. Dec. 168 (1983) decided on a motion to dismiss and without determining the merits of the claim.

65. Siemieniec v. Luthern General Hospital, 134 Ill. App. 3d 823, 480 N.E. 2d 1227, 89 Ill. Dec. 484 (1985).

66. Tay-Sachs disease is a fatal, progressive, degenerative disease of the nervous system which occurs primarily in Jewish infants of eastern European ancestry. A diseased child appears normal at birth, but a four to six months of age, the child's central nervous system begins to degenerate, and he suffers eventual blindness, deafness, paralysis, seizures, and mental retardation. His life expectancy is two to four years. Only in the circumstances where both parents are carriers of the Tay-Sachs trait will there be a great likelihood of the presence of the disease in their offspring. The carrier is not affected by the disease, but if both parents are carriers, the probability that their child will have the disease is one in four. There is a blood test to identify carriers of the Tay-Sachs trait. If tests show that both parents are carriers, an amniocentesis can be performed to determine whether the fetus is afflicted with the disease. Goldberg ex cel. Goldberg v. Ruskin, 128 Ill. App 3d 1029, 471 N.E. 2d 530, 84 Ill. Dec. 1, 3 n2 (1984).

67. Adapted from Goldberg ex cel. Goldberg v. Ruskin, 128 Ill. App. 3d 1029, 471 N.E. 2d 530, 84 Ill. Dec. 1 (1984) decided on a motion to dismiss and without determining the merits of the claim.

68. Id.

69. Goldberg ex cel. Goldberg v. Ruskin, 128 Ill. App. 3d 1029 471 N.E. 2d 530, 84 Ill. Dec. 1, (1984).

70. Adapted from Siemieniec v. Lutheran General Hospital, 134 Ill. App 3d 823, 480 N.E. 2d 1227, 89 Ill. Dec. 484 (1985) decided on a motion to dismiss and without determining the merits of the claim.

71. Information regarding federal law can be obtained from the United States Department of Justice, Registration Section, P.O. Box 28083, Central Station, Drug Enforcement Administration, Washington, DC 20005, or by telephoning its Chicago office at (312) 353-7889. The Drug Enforcement Substance Act of 1970 – A Manual for the Medical Practitioner" which should be reviewed by every practitioner.

72. Ohligschlager v. Proctor Community Hospital, 55 Ill. 2d 411, 303 N.E. 2d 392 (1973).

73. Kirk v. Michael Reese Hospital and Medical Center, 136 Ill. App. 3d 945, 483 N.E. 2d 1319, 64 Ill. Dec. 511 (1982).

74. See Magana v. Elie, 108 Ill, App. 3d 1028, 439 N.E. 2d 1319, 64 Ill. Dec. 511 (1982).

75. Id.

76. Id.

77. No claim was made against the general practitioner, but the oral surgeon in defense sought to establish that steroids and penicillin was not the medically preferred treatment. The court noted that although the treatment may have been improper and counter productive under the circumstances, it did not insulate the oral surgeon from liability, particularly since he admitted that had he seen Jean, he probably could have treated her abscess effectively.

78. Adapted from Longman v. Jasiek, 91 Ill App. 3d 83, 414 N.E. 2d 520, 46 Ill. Dec. 636 (1980) $35,000 awarded.

79. S. Warren & L. Brandeis, The Right to Privacy, 4 Harv. L. Rev. 193 (1980).

80. JCAH Accreditation Manual for Hospitals at ____ (1985).

81. 735 Illinois Compiled Statutes 5/8-802.

82. See 325 Illinois Compiled Statutes 5/1 et seg.

83. Illinois Compiled Statutes 5/8-802.

84. Illinois Revised Statutes, ch. 91 ½, par. 801 et seg.

85. Id.

86. Edwards ex cel. Phillips v. University of Chicago Hospitals and Clinics. ____ Ill. App. 3d ___, 484 N.E. 2d 1100, 92 Ill. Dec. 245 (1985).

87. Id.

88. Id.

89. Edwards v. University of Chicago Hospitals and Clinics. ___Ill. App. 3d___, 484 N. E. 2d 1100, 92 Ill. Dec. 245 (1985).

90. Adapted from Tarasoff v. Regents of the Univ. of Cal. 17 Cal. 3d 425, 551 P.2d 334, 131 Cal. Rptr. 14 (1976).

91. Smith v. Kurtzman, 106 Ill. App. 3d 712, 436 N.E.2d 1. 62 Ill. Dec. 419, (1982).

92. Knierim v. Izzo, 22 Ill. 2d 73, 174 N.E. 2d 157 (1961) (intentional): Rickey v. Chicago Transit Authority, 98 Ill. 2d 54, 457 N.E. 2d 1. 75 Ill. Dec. 211 (1982) (negligent).

93. 146. Knierim v. Izzo, 22 Ill. 2d 73, 174 N.E. 2d 157 (1961).

94. Dymek v. Nyquiest, 128 Ill. App. 3d 859, 469 N.E. 2d 659, 83 Ill. Dec. 52 (1984).

95. Rickey v. Chicago Transit Authority, 98 Ill. 2d 546, 457 N.E.2d 1. 75 Ill. Dec. 211 (1983). This case involved a claim by Robert Rickey to recover damages for emotional distress allegedly suffered when he viewed an accidental injury to his brother, Richard, who, with Robert, was standing on a descending escalator. Part of Richard's clothing became entangled in the mechanism at the base of the escalator, and he was choked and could breathe for a substantial period of time. A comatose condition resulted.

96. See Siemieniec v. Luthern General Hospital, 134 Ill. App. 3d 823, 480 N.E. 2d 1227, 89 Ill. Dec. 484 (1985): Golberg v. Ruskin, 128 Ill. App. 3d 1029, 471 N.E. 2d 530, 84 Ill. Dec. 1 (1984).

97. See Phillips v. United States, 575 F. Supp. 1309 (D.S.C. 1983): Harbeson v. Parke-Davis, Inc., 98 Wash. 2d 460, 656 P.2d 483 (1983); Speck v. Finegold, 497 Pa. 77, 439 A.2d 110 (1981); Berman v. Allan, 80 N.J. 421, 404 A.2d 8 (1979); Eisbrenner v. Stanley, 106 Mich. App. 357, 308 N.W. 2d 209 (1981).

98. Gihring v. Butcher. ____Ill. App. 3d ___, 487 N.E. 2d 75, 93 ILL. Dec. 631 (1985).

99. W. Keeton, Prosser and Keeton on The Law of Torts at 47 (5ᵗʰ ed., 1984).

100. See below for discussion of future forms of medical malpractice.

101. See below for disussion of consents regarding minors.

102. Adapted from Horak v. Biris, 130 Ill. App. 3d 140, 474 N.E. 2d 13, 85 Ill. Dec. 599 (1985).

103. M. Belli. Belli For Your Malpractice Defense at 202 (Medical Economics Books, Oradell, N.J., 1986)

104. Id. at 203.

105. Id at 204.

106. Id at 205
107. Id. at 206
108. Id at 210.

Chapter IV

1. Asher v. Stromberg. ____Ill. App. 2d ___ 223 N.E. 2d 300 (1966).
2. M. Twin, et al, and Humor of the Age at 383 (Star Publications Co., Chicago, Ill. 1882).
3. 71 ABA Journal at 38 (December, 1985) (comments of Grant P. DuBois).
4. Illinois Revised Statutes, ch. 110A, Canon 2, Rule 2-106©.
5. Id
6. Id.
7. Snyder v. Lowrey, ___Ill, App. 3d ___, 489 N.E. 2d 899, 95 Ill. Dec. 337 (1986). The court did not have before it the merits of the claim. What the court did was to order Lowrey to reveal the names of all attorneys who had referred cases to him during the past ten years, the names of all persons so referred and the division of fees.
8. Illinois Revised Statutes, ch. 110, par. 8-2001. An exception is made for certain mental health records. See Illinois Revised Statutes, ch 110, par. 8-2004.
9. Id.
10. Illinois Revised Statutes, ch 110, par. 8-2003. Clinical psychologists records are generally not subject to examination unless the clinical psychologist consents or examination is authorized by a court. Illinois Revised Statutes, ch. 110, par. 8-2004.
11. Standard of care is discussed in a previous chapter in greater detail.
12. This topic is discussed in more detail in a previous chapter.
13. M. Belli. Belli for Your Malpractice Defense at 8 and 207 (Medical Economics Co., Inc. (1986).
14. 72 ABA Journal at 119 (April, 1986).
15. W. Keeton, Prosser and Keeton on The Law of Tort at 243 (5th Ed., 1984).
16. Id.
17. Walker v. Rumer, 72 Ill. 2d 495, 381 N.E. 2d 689, 21 Ill. Dec. 362 (1978).
18. Spidle v. Steward, 79 Ill. 2d 1, 402 N.E. 2d 1, 402 N.E. 2d 216, 37 Ill. Dec. 326 (1980).
19. Illinois Revised Statutes, ch. 110, par. 2-1113.
20. Kolakowski v. Voris, 83 Ill. 2d 388, 415 N.E. 2d 397, 47 Ill. Dec. 392 (1980).
21. Metz v. Fairbury Hospital, 118. Ill. App. 3d 1093, 455 N.E.2d 1096, 74 Ill. Dec. 472, (1983); Comie v. O'Neil, 125 Ill. App. 2d 450, 261 N.E. 2d 21 (1970).
22. Cassady v. Hendrickson, ___Ill. App. 3d___, 486 N.E. 2d 1329, 93 Ill. Dec. 494 (1985).
23. 33 Ill. 2d 326, 211 N.E. 2d 253 (1965).
24. U.S. Const. Art Ill. Sec. 2. See also 28 U.S.C. sec. 1331.

Chapter V

1. An excellent book to read about the psychological impact of being sued for medical malpractice is Defendant, a Psychiatrist on Trial for Medical Malpractice by Sara C. Charles, M.D.
2. See Illinois Revised Statutes, ch 110A, par. 101
3. See Illinois Revised Statutes, ch 110A par 104

4. Although a parent automatically has custody of a child he is not automatically in charge of his estate or money. He must be appointed to also have charge of the child's money or estate. See Illinois Revised Statutes, Ch. 110 ½, par. 11-1 et seg.

Chapter VI

1. See Ch. V for discussion of the statute of limitations.
2. Illinois Revised Statutes, ch 110, par. 2-622. See Chapter V. Section 1 (e) for a discussion of the affidavit requirement.
3. Illinois Revised Statutes, ch 111, par 4404, provides that: Any person licensed pursuant to this Act (relating to the licensing of physicians) or any other state or territory in the United States, except a person licensed to practice midwifery, who in good faith and without prior notice of the illness or injury provides emergency care without fee to a person, shall not, as a result of his acts or omissions, except willful or wanton misconduct on the part of such persons, in providing such care, be liable for civil damages.
4. Illinois Revised Statutes, ch. 111, par. 4405.
5. Several other statutes include, but are not limited to doctors. They include the Emergency Medical Services Systems Act which exempts from liability services related to pre-hospital emergency medical services, including paramedic units, such as giving radio instructions to mobile units or emergency sites. (Illinois Revised Statutes, ch. 111 ½, par. 5501 et seg.); the Choke-Saving Methods Act which exempts from liability persons aiding a choking person (Illinois Revised Statutes, ch. 56 ½, par. 601 et seg); and a statute which exempts from liability persons who have completed a cardiopulmonary resuscitation (CPR) course if they therefore provide emergency services (Illinois Revised Statutes. Ch. 111 ½, par.871).
6. Alvis v. Riber, 85 Ill, 2d 1. 421 N.E. 2d 886, 52 Ill. Dec. 23, (1981).

Chapter VII
1. According to the Rules of the Illinois Supreme Court, a pretrial conference is held to consider: (1) the simplification of the issues; (2) amendments to the pleadings; (3) the possibility of obtaining admission of fact and of documents which will avoid unnecessary proof; (4) the limitation of the number of expert witnesses; and (5) any other matter which may aid in the disposition of the action. Illinois Revised Statutes, ch. 110A, par. 218.
2. Before action is taken, the doctor is allowed the opportunity to respond to the report.
3. Black's Law Dictionary (4th Ed.) at 174d.
4. One book discussing these techniques is written by doctor-lawyer William J. Bryan, Jr., entitled The Chosen Ones or (The Psychology of Jury Selection), published by Vantage Press.
5. The instructions quoted are from Illinois and are published in Illinois Pattern Jury Instructions. Civil prepared by the Illinois Supreme Court Committee on Jury Instructions.
6. See Chapter II regarding the standard of care of doctors.
7. IPI No. 105.1.
8. IPI No. 105.2
9. IPI No. 105.3
10. See Chapter III for a discussion of liability for borrowed servants.
11. IPI No. 105.04.
12. See Chapter III regarding consent.
13. IPI No. 105.05.
14. IPS No. 105.07.
15. IPI No. 105.06.
16. IPI No. 105.06. Because of comparative negligence, the patient's negligence may only reduce the damages claimed.
17. See Chapter IV regarding the Illinois Judicial System

APPENDIX B

PUBLICATIONS FROM DO-IT-YOURSELF LEGAL PUBLISHERS/SELFHELPER LAW PRESS

The following is a list of publications from the Do-it-YourselfLegal Publishers/Selfhelper Law Press of America. (**Customers:** For your convenience, just make a photocopy of this page and send it along with your order. All prices quoted here are subject to change without notice.)

1. How To Draw Up Your Own Friendly Separation/Property Settlement Agreement With Your Spouse
2. Tenant Smart: How To Win Your Tenants' Legal Rights Without A Lawyer (New York Edition)
3. How To Probate & Settle An Estate Yourself Without The Lawyers' Fees ($35)
4. How To Adopt A Child Without A Lawyer
5. How To Form Your Own Profit/Non-Profit Corporation Without A Lawyer
6. How To Plan Your Total' Estate With A Will & Living Will, Without a Lawyer
7. How To Declare Your Personal Bankruptcy Without A Lawyer ($29)
8. How To Buy Or Sell Your Own Home Without A Lawyer or Broker ($29)
9. How To File For Chapter 11 Business Bankruptcy Without A Lawyer ($29)
10. How To Legally Beat The Traffic Ticket Without A Lawyer (forthcoming)
11. How To Settle Your Own Auto Accident Claims Without A Lawyer ($29.95)
12. How To Obtain Your U.S. Immigration Visa Without A Lawyer ($31.95)
13. How To Do Your Own Divorce Without A Lawyer [10 Regional State-Specific Volumes] ($35)
14. How To Legally Change Your Name Without A Lawyer ($26.95)
15. How To Properly Plan Your Total' Estate With A Living Trust, Without The Lawyers' Fees ($35)
16. Legally Protect Yourself In A Gay/Lesbian Or Non-Marital Relationship With A Cohabitation Agreement
17. Before You Say 'I do' In Marriage Or Co-Habitation, Here's How To First Protect Yourself Legally
18. The National Home Mortgage Escrow Audit Kit (forthcoming) ($15.95)

Prices: Each book, *except* for those specifically priced otherwise, costs $28, plus $5.00 per book for postage and handling. New Jersey residents please add 6% sales tax. **ALL PRICES ARE SUBJECT TO CHANGE WITHOUT NOTICE**

ORDER FORM

CUSTOMERS: Please make and send a photo copy of this page with your orders) TO: Do-it-Yourself Legal
Publishers
27 Edgarton Terrace
East Orange, NJ 07017

Please send me the following:
1. _____ copies of _____
2. _____ copies of _____
3. _____ copies of _____
4. _____ copies of _____

Enclosed is the sum of $_____ to cover the order. *Mail my order to:*
Mr./Mrs.//Ms/Dr. _____ _____
Address (include Zip Code please): _____
Phone No. and area code: (   ) _____ Job: (   ) _____
*New Jersey residents enclose 6% sales tax.

IMPORTANT: Please do NOT rip out the page. Consider others! Just make a photocopy and send it.

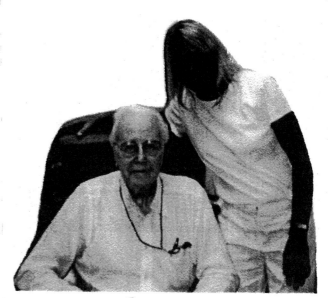

Author Roy T. Rapp, M.D., with Judy Hackworth,
the author's writing assistant , and Senior Nurse, Rapp Clinic.

About the Author

Roy Thomas Rapp, is a graduate of the University of Illinois College of Medicine, Chicago, Illinois, and a board-certified physician in both the American Board of Family Practice and the American Board of Abdominal Surgery in active practice for the past 50 years. Dr. Rapp has garnered many distinguished awards and honors from peers and patients, alike, for his long and unblemished medical career, especially distinguished by his singular dedication to his patients, and, in turn, for their love and fondness for him. The latest one of such awards, is the 2004 "Distinguished Service Award" made to Dr. Rapp by the Illinois Academy of Family Physicians in May 2004.

He has written over 4 dozen articles on various issues of medicine in many prestigious medical journals, including the *American Journal of Nursing, the West Virginia Medical Journal, the Journal of Abdominal Surgery, the Modern Medicine, the Annals of Long Term Care,* among many others, and is the co-author of the book, *Illinois Medical Malpractice – A Guide for Health Sciences*, published by C.V. Mosby Company. Of his current authorship of *SO YOU REALLY WANT TO SUE YOUR DOCTOR!,* a close member of his family who has known Dr. Rapp right from infancy, says of him, "No surprise there. He has always maintained an interest in both law and medicine."

Dr. Rapp is a dedicated family man whose prime love and pride is his beloved wife and children. Married to his present wife, Lucille, since 1943, he is the proud father of 6 children, five of whom are attorneys, and 13 grandchildren. Of these five attorney-sons, one of them is both an attorney and a physician.

111

INDEX